Science Is Fun!

For Families and Classroom Groups

Science Is Fun!

For Families and Classroom Groups

CAROL OPPENHEIM

𝒞 CRACOM CORPORATION

St. Louis, Missouri

Published by CRACOM Corporation
12131 Dorsett Road, Maryland Heights, Missouri 63043

Computer Graphics: Judith A. Schmitt

Notice: The reader is warned expressly to consider and adopt all safety precautions that might be indicated by the activities described herein and to avoid all potential hazards. By following the instructions contained herein, the reader willingly assumes all risks in connection with such instructions.

Library of Congress Cataloging-in-Publication Data

Oppenheim, Carol.
    Science is fun! : for families and classroom groups / Carol
Oppenheim.
        p.   cm.
    Includes index.
    ISBN 0-9633555-1-1
    1. Science--Study and teaching (Early childhood)--United States.
I. Title.
LB1139.5.S35067   1993
372.3'5'0973--dc20   92-35717
                                                                            CIP
                                                                            AC

Printed in the United States of America

Last digit is the print number: 10   9   8   7   6   5   4   3   2   1

This book is lovingly dedicated
to
my grandmother, Sallie Lehman,
who took my hand and showed me the wildflowers,
to
my husband, Art,
for his love and encouragement through the years,
and
in memory of our son, Jim,
who loved the outdoors.

About the Author

Carol Oppenheim is a teacher, wife, mother, and grandmother who enjoys sharing her interest in nature and science with both children and adults. She received her Bachelor of Arts degree in Child Study from Webster University and has also earned Child Development Associate certification. In 1992 Carol was a winner in Citicorp's Innovative Teacher Contest.

After teaching preschool for many years, Carol developed a science curriculum she calls *Science Is Fun!* For seven years she used this curriculum while serving as a "traveling teacher" before joining the staff of the Forsyth School in St. Louis, Missouri, as a science specialist in 1991. Carol teaches adults as well when she conducts teacher and parent workshops.

Carol is a member of the Association for the Education of Young Children and is a volunteer naturalist at Rockwoods Reservation, Missouri Department of Conservation.

Reviewers

The following individuals have reviewed specific content areas.
Their constructive criticisms and suggestions have been invaluable
in ensuring accurate and up-to-date material.

Cathy de Jong
Forest Area Manager
Missouri Department of Conservation
St. Louis, Missouri

Cynthia D. Fauser
Food and Nutrition Specialist
University Extension
University of Missouri System
St. Louis, Missouri

K. James Ferguson
Volunteer, Botany Department
Missouri Botanical Garden
St. Louis, Missouri

Judy Higgins
Assistant Nature Center Manager
Missouri Department of Conservation
St. Louis, Missouri

Skip Kincaid
Skip Kincaid & Associates
Forestry Consultants
Urban Forestry and Timber Management
St. Louis, Missouri

Ann P. McMahon
Creative Perspectives
St. Louis, Missouri

Dave Murray
Chief Meteorologist
KTVI Television
St. Louis, Missouri

Acknowledgments

Science Is Fun! was written as a response to the many parents and teachers who ask me, "How do you get the children so turned on to science?"

Turning the **idea** of writing a book called *Science Is Fun!* into the **reality** of a finished book was certainly a team effort.

I am sincerely grateful to each of the reviewers listed on page ix for the time and effort they generously contributed.

In addition, I deeply appreciate all the help I received from the following people:

Carol Kaplan, who has always encouraged me in both my teaching and my writing.

Craig Cuddeback, who offered me the challenge of writing this book.

Judy Schmitt and Cynthia D. Cooney, who created the meaningful illustrations that bring life and joy to the words.

Mary Espenschied, who helped me organize my ideas and taught me to write without exclamation marks!

Nancy Ladousier, who turned my handwritten scribbles into legible type.

Bette Russ, for the lovely cover design.

Andrew Espenschied, Satomi Fujii, Amber Haire, and Evan Hume, for being with me in the cover photo.

Becky Bopp, for allowing us to use her classroom while taking the photo.

Children, who give me a reason to continue exploring, collecting, saving, learning, teaching, and writing.

This turtle is my logo. You will find it throughout the book.

If you have suggestions about how to make *Science Is Fun!* more helpful or ideas and other suggested readings to add, please contact me through the publisher.

CAROL OPPENHEIM

Contents

Science Is Fun!

For Families and Classroom Groups

June 5, '93
Saw a
June bug
today

June 8, '93
The baby
robins
are out of
the nest!

Chapter 1

How to Use This Book

STARCH

FACT

To enjoy *Science Is Fun!* you don't have to "know about science," but you do need to be **curious, young at heart,** and **ready for fun.**

I sincerely believe that one of the greatest gifts you can give a child is a love and appreciation of our world. In this time of computers, television, video games, battery-operated toys, and instant everything, it is more vital than ever to explore the *real world* with children. Rachel Carson wrote—

> If I had influence with the good fairy I should ask her that her gift to each child in the world be a sense of wonder so indestructible that it would last throughout life, as an unfailing antidote against the boredom and disenchantments of later years, the sterile preoccupation with things that are artificial, the alienation from the sources of our strength.

Children are naturally curious. They need opportunities for exploration and the companionship of at least one adult with whom to share the joy and excitement of new discoveries. In *Science for Young Children*, Viola Carmichael wrote —

> Science should be discovery rather than memorization of facts. As the child watches, wonders, studies and questions, he is experiencing science as a part of everyday living.

Science Is Fun! is a book for adults and children of all ages to enjoy together. It *suggests* fun, simple ways to observe, appreciate, and learn about nature and science. It *offers* exciting opportunities for children and adults to talk, play, and learn *together.* It *awakens* a sense of wonder in all ages and *encourages* older children to try the activities themselves, share the fun with friends, and help younger sisters, brothers, or friends enjoy nature and science.

It is my hope that the children and adults using this book will find that exciting things will happen, that they will—

- See the world with "new eyes"
- Share many new experiences
- Explore new places and ideas
- Touch many items
- Guess and wonder

- Notice likes and differences
- Make comparisons
- Look things up in books
- Learn new words
- Hear different sounds
- Express their thoughts
- Talk and write about things they have seen and done
- Discuss size, shape, color, number
- Pretend and act out
- Laugh and enjoy
- See the world with a new sense of wonder
- Gain a deeper love and appreciation of our world
- Share the responsibility for caring for our world
- And, also discover that *Science Is Fun!*

My main hope is that this book will help adults and children find new interests to share and provide hours of pleasure as they spend time together.

CAROL OPPENHEIM

HELPFUL HINTS FOR ADULTS

- To begin, read all this introductory material first. It will just take a few minutes and will tell you easy, fun ways to enjoy this book and its activities.
- Take a good look at chapter 2, Exploring—Collecting—Saving, to discover enjoyable ways to begin your adventures. All ages will find ideas to try.

  As you explore, take good care of the earth and its creatures (see Guidelines for Thoughtful Collecting, page 15).
- Talk about guidelines for safety, but ***try not to pass on unfounded fears*** you may have learned as a small child.
- Pick a chapter that appeals to you and the children and begin to have fun. Just relax—there is no pressure to do it all in one day!

- Notice that interesting ⧼FA⧸CTS⧽ are "sprinkled" throughout each chapter. Children love facts, so be sure to share these bits of knowledge with them.

- Be sure to *let the children do* as much as possible—not just watch you do things. *Remember:* When I hear I forget. When I see I remember. **When I do I learn!**

    Little hands and feet are sometimes slow and awkward, but each attempt (when encouraged by a caring adult or older child) is a giant step forward in learning and will help to establish a positive self-concept in the child.

- As you use the ideas in *Science Is Fun!,* you will often be following the *scientific method,* which includes—

    1. Gathering facts and needed materials
    2. Setting up the experiment
    3. Predicting outcomes
    4. Hands-on observations
    5. Recording observations
    6. Sharing knowledge with others
    7. Reaching conclusions and planning for the experiment's closure.

- Help the children feel that *"it's fun to try something new,"* that *"I'm getting better or I'm good at this."* Listen to the children's ideas. They will feel that "What I say really matters!" Decide together what to do, whenever possible. Teamwork is terrific. Adults and children working and playing together—that is what counts.

- Realize that *how a finished product looks* (such as a leaf rubbing) *is not important! Having good feelings and doing things together are important!*

- Make gluing projects easy! Pour a little glue (or paste) into a small container and use popsicle sticks to apply it. Show the children how to put a *little* glue on each piece to be glued down. Also, cover the table with newspaper for easy clean up.

    When a child creates a picture, instead of saying, "What is it?" it is helpful to say, "Would you like to tell me about your picture?" The child may say "No" or may give you a whole story about his or her creation! Children *sometimes* like for you to print *their exact words* on the picture or on a separate piece of paper. This is easy and fun and has prereading and language benefits as well! *Remember:* you may not see the "tree" or other recognizable object in a child's picture. It may be lines or circles to you, but to the child it may represent a certain thing. Art work you can "recognize" evolves slowly and naturally *without anyone's teaching the child to draw.*

■ Consider beginning a Science/Nature Book Collection. (See Helpful Resources, page 6.) Look for great bargains in books of all kinds at garage sales. Keep a Science Record Book (a spiral notebook works well) or make notes on a special Science Calendar. When adults and children make a written record of things they have collected or grown or seen, they will have a diary of interesting happenings, will get in the habit of observing everything more closely, and will learn how to write down observations (and perhaps sometimes make rough sketches) of things they want to remember. When possible, let the children help with the writing and drawing.

Our Memory Book

June 5, '93
Saw a June bug today

June 8, '93
The baby robins are out of the nest!

JUNE

SUN	MON	TUES	WED	THURS	FRI	SAT
1 Planted lima bean	2	3	4	5 Bean came up!	6	7
8	9 Found a beetle	10	11	12	13	14
15	16	17	18	19	20 Saw a rainbow	21
22 / 29	23 / 30	24	25	26	27	28

A Science Record Book allows you to write down things in as much detail as you wish. For example,

February 16, 1993: Pulled 6 kernels off an ear of Indian corn and planted them in a plastic glass.

February 22: All 6 corn seeds are up today!

February 25: A downy woodpecker came to our suet feeder for the first time today.

February 30: The corn plants are 8 inches tall now! Lots of white roots are showing in the soil.

March 15: We forgot to water our corn, and it is dead. We will bury the soil, roots, and dead plants in our compost pile (see page 160) and plant more corn in the cup.

A Science Calendar is also fun but has room only for short comments.

- Remember that items like science or nature books, bug keepers, special shells, and a magnifying glass make wonderful gifts for children.

- Pretend together. Children love to pretend. When children "act out" or pretend, they take on the roll, learn new facts, remember, and also have an opportunity to move their bodies. They keep interested and involved in what is going on. In this book you will see suggestions to "act out" being a butterfly, a tree, and other things in nature. Adults and children enjoy pretending together.

- When you become interested and decide to read more about a certain subject, you will probably make the same discovery I did—all resources do not agree. Then you will understand why I love the birdwatcher's proverb: *When the bird and the book disagree, always believe the bird!*

HELPFUL RESOURCES

- Reference and fiction books in your public library children's section. The librarian will help you find helpful books on many topics and show older children how to use the card catalog so they can help themselves.

- The *World Book Encyclopedia:* contains background facts presented in a clear, interesting way.

- *Ranger Rick* and *Your Big Back Yard:* excellent magazines. Write:

    National Wildlife Federation

    1400 Sixteenth Street, N.W.

    Washington, DC 20036-2266

    or call 1-800-432-6564 for information.

- *Books For Young Explorers:* wonderful nature books for young children. Write:

    National Geographic Education Services

    Washington, DC 20036

    or call 1-800-638-4077 for information.

- *Golden Nature Guide Series* (Racine, Wisconsin: Western Publishing Co.): books are available at most book stores. They contain good pictures and basic facts to help with identification. Some of the many titles are *Birds, Insects, Trees,* and *Seashores.*

- *Science In A Nutshell:* good basic information—easy to understand. Write:

    Kimbo Educational

    P.O. Box 477

    Long Branch, NJ 07740.

- *Science Experiences for Young Children* by Viola Carmichael (Saratoga, California: R&E Publishers, 1982).

- City and County Parks: call for locations of parks and activities available.

- State Department of Conservation or Natural Resources: free magazines, maps, and educational materials are often available. Call the numbers listed in the blue pages of your phone book for information or write direct to the department at your state capital.

- National Parks of the United States: Write:

    National Park Service

    Attention: Office of Public Affairs

    U.S. Department of the Interior

    P.O. Box 37127

    Washington, DC 20013-7127

- Poison Center: for preventive care and emergency help. See your phone book and keep the phone number on every phone.

- The following groups offer free informative booklets:

    American Heart Association

    American Lung Association

    American Cancer Society

    Chamber of Commerce

- Neighbors, friends, teachers, grandparents, and other family members may share your interests and provide information.

Chapter 2
Exploring
Collecting
Saving

Come forth into the light of things, let nature be your teacher.

WILLIAM WORDSWORTH

An interest in science must be caught more than taught! You don't need to be an expert—just interested. I define **nature** as everything in the world that is natural—not "person made"—and **science** as just a more organized look at nature.

EXPLORING

Exploring is an adventure for young and old. You never know what you will find or what will happen.

EXPLORING ALLOWS EVERYONE TO—

- See the world with "new eyes."
- Appreciate our wonderful world and remember not to take it for granted.
- Observe, discover, and learn together.
- Build lasting memories—"Remember the time we took a night walk to listen for owls—or found the turtle shell—or smelled the skunk?"

BEFORE YOU BEGIN EXPLORING—

- Discuss the rules for *safety* and *good manners.* (Remind everyone to ask permission before going on other people's property.)
- Warn children that they MUST *NOT* TASTE berries,

leaves, and so on because SOME ARE POISON. (See Helpful Resources, page 7.)

- Decide together which special things to look for as you explore. For example, "Let's take a walk and see how many red flowers or different kinds of birds we can find."

- Decide whether to take a listening walk or a smelling walk or a collecting walk.

- Think about recording anything special in your Science Record Book or Calendar. (See page 4.) This is a very meaningful activity because it allows you to write down nature or science events that are important to your family or class and to look back later when you want to recall the details of a certain event.

- Check other sections of this book for many other ideas.

AS YOU EXPLORE, *ENJOY!*

Look—Listen—Touch—Smell. Talk about things being bumpy—smooth—sticky—pretty—strange—alike—different—big—little—wild—tame—colorful—dull—and *amazing.*

Remember to visit the same places in spring, summer, fall, and winter in order to notice differences and appreciate the change of seasons.

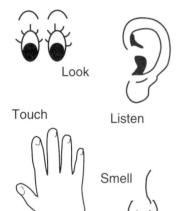

Explore Your Own Yard and Neighborhood

YOU MAY DISCOVER

 Creatures under rocks and in the grass, bees around the flowers, dead insects, earthworms

underground, plants you never noticed before, four-leaf clovers, birds, feathers, nests, woodpecker holes, wild and pet animals, trees, seeds, roots, galls (see page 32), signs of spring, summer, fall, winter, and what else?

Explore Your Local, State, and National Parks and Forests

Prepare for this type of exploring by using insect repellent and by asking a forest ranger or conservation agent to help you recognize things to avoid such as poison ivy, poison oak, and nettle.

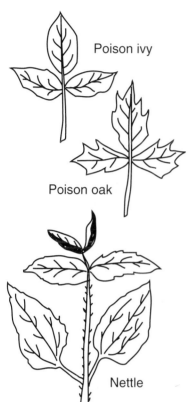

Poison ivy

Poison oak

Nettle

The adventure involved is fun and gives everyone a chance to practice being patient and being a good sport.

YOU MAY DISCOVER

All the items found in your yard and neighborhood plus rocks, fossils, nuts, ferns, moss, fungus, wildflowers, turtles, turtle shells, snakes, snake skins, lizards, snails, fallen trees, animals skulls and bones, animal feces, natural forest litter (decaying leaves etc.), and if you are lucky, a glimpse of wild creatures such as turkey, deer, or fox, and if you are unlucky, litter left by people, ticks, chiggers, poison ivy, or poison oak. Don't let the negatives bother you because *exploring in the woods is a special treat.*

Explore Ponds, Rivers, Creeks, Streams, and Lakes

Prepare by being sure that the children are closely supervised. Everyone should WEAR LIFE JACKETS when needed.

YOU MAY DISCOVER

Fish, turtles, snakes, salamanders, toads, frogs, shells, water birds, dragonflies, cattails, clams, crayfish, water insects, wildlife coming for water, bats feeding at dusk, and what else?

If you sit quietly by the water or walk slowly near the water's edge, you may see many amazing creatures— some hiding just below the water. (Look up *camouflage*.)

Explore The Ocean Shoreline

Prepare by borrowing library books about ocean life. Perhaps buy *Beach Book* by Karen Dawe (Workman Publishing, New York) or *Seashores* from the *Golden Nature Guide Series.* Be sure to WEAR SUNSCREEN. When visiting the ocean be sure to look carefully for life in the tide pools, which are shallow pools left behind when the tide is low. Try to find out more about tide pools from books or from someone who knows about them. The living things found in tide pools are fascinating.

YOU MAY DISCOVER

Sand, driftwood, shells, hermit crabs, beach birds, fish, seaweed, jellyfish,

crabs, sand dollars, starfish, and much, much more.

Watch the Sky

Spread an old cover on the ground, lie down, and watch the sky. (Warn children that THEY MUST NOT LOOK AT THE SUN.)

YOU MAY DISCOVER

Beautiful clouds, clear sky, clouds moving before your eyes, clouds that look like people or things, signs of a storm, a rainbow, insects, birds, planes, jet streams, and what else? (See Rainbows, page 135.) Try this same idea at night and listen for night sounds too! If you are very lucky, you may hear owls, whippoorwills, or the honking sounds of migrating Canada Geese.

An Adventure At Dusk

In a bird book look up *chimney swift*.

- Chimney swifts build their nests on a vertical surface inside chimneys or hollow trees with twigs glued together with their sticky saliva.
- Their feet are so small they cannot stand or perch but must rest clinging to a rough surface.
- They spend most of their lives in the air—eating insects, drinking, bathing, and gathering nesting materials while in flight!

Now explore your neighborhood for a school or other large building with an uncapped chimney. Go there at dusk, sit down, and watch the show. Isn't a chimney swift an interesting bird?

Explore Caves

Caves are great fun to explore but you MUST BE GUIDED BY AN EXPERT. (See Bats, page 87.)

COLLECTING

It has been said, "Take only photographs; leave only footprints." However, people (especially children) love to collect things. Children learn by using all five senses. Collecting encourages looking, touching, smelling, and hearing many interesting things. Family and class collections encourage children and adults to talk about a shared interest as they decide together what to collect—where to look—when to go—where to keep the collection.

Remember: You do not need to collect things every time you go exploring to enjoy the exploration. But if you are like I am, you will have a plastic bag for collecting tucked away in your pocket—just in case you discover some unexpected treasure.

Collecting can be a joy without upsetting nature's balance if everyone is a thoughtful, caring collector.

The guidelines for collecting in your own yard will be somewhat different than for other places because in your yard the adults will set the rules about picking flowers and what things are out of bounds. However, the following basic guidelines for thoughtful collecting will apply to all the places you may go.

Guidelines for Thoughtful Collecting

First check with your local, state, and national park and forest officials to see what rules they might have about collecting.

- DO NOT pick or dig up living plants. Enjoy looking at ferns, moss, and wildflowers but leave them as you found them for others to see. To reproduce they must be left in place to drop their seeds and spores. (Look up *spores*.) Is this a new word for you?

- NEVER take home a living, wild creature. ***Wild animals do not make good pets.*** They often die in captivity and want only to be free. It is not kind to confine wild creatures. It is fun to examine, touch, even smell a turtle, but then put it right back where it was. If you want to watch a live insect or spider in a bug keeper (see page 49), be sure to let it go after a short while so it will not die. ***Having respect for the lives of all creatures is important.***

- DO look for unattached, interesting items you may want to collect.

Examples of Collectible Items

Acorn

Acorns and nuts (just a few since animals need them for food), galls (see page 32), a *few* rocks (many people are collecting them), turtle shells, snake skins, empty snail shells, dead insects, leaves, pine cones, loose bark, animal bones, and sea shells. (See other chapters for ideas.) For collection and identification purposes, take small pieces of tree branches with leaves and seed pods.

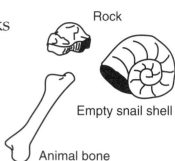

Rock

Empty snail shell

Animal bone

Leaf

Seed pods

What To Take Along When Collecting

- *Sunscreen and insect repellent.*
- *Water* in a screw-top pill bottle in everyone's pocket and lots of water for long explorations. *Snacks.*

- *Collecting bag* with handles. Children can draw on paper bags like this.
- *Plastic bag:* tuck one in your pocket if you want free hands.
- Optional: magnifying glass, binoculars, *Golden Nature Guide* books.

SAVING

MARY'S BOX

OUR BEETLE BOX

Where shall we put all these treasures we have collected? Having a special place for your treasures makes collecting more meaningful and fun and also makes housekeeping much easier.

IDEAS THAT WORK

- Have a special *shelf* or *tray* for displaying your nature treasures. This might hold newly found or special treasures and should be easily available for all ages (except toddlers!) to see and touch. The children may want to take turns caring for this display. They learn to handle fragile items with care. This collection will change as new items are added and old ones are stored away. What a great display to show to visitors!

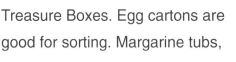

- *Treasure boxes:* Produce departments have sturdy boxes (lime, tomato, etc.) with nice flat lids in various sizes. Ask your produce clerk to save some for you. Children can help paint (any indoor or outdoor house paint will work) and decorate these boxes using stickers and their own drawings or pictures cut from nature magazines and glued on. Markers can be used for lettering.

    Gift idea: Treasure boxes with a magnifying glass, a *Golden Nature Guide* book, and a few nature items tucked inside make a nice gift.

- Smaller boxes with lids can be used to store treasures and then put away inside your larger Treasure Boxes. Egg cartons are good for sorting. Margarine tubs, jewelry boxes, and boxes with clear plastic lids are great for displaying your insect collection. (See Creepy, Crawly Creatures, page 48.)

Continued.

 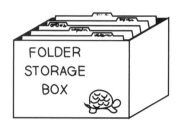

- ***Nature scrapbooks and folders:*** Pressed flowers and leaves, pictures cut from magazines, newspaper articles and pictures, or pictures drawn by children and adults can be saved in scrapbooks. Scrapbooks can be made from any kind of paper, with construction paper covers and metal rings as fasteners, or folders can be made by folding large construction paper or poster board in half. You may want a different folder for each subject. It is easy to add more pages to folders. They can be stored on edge in a box that is slightly wider than the folders. Keep them from falling over with a brick or something heavy until your Folder Box begins to fill up.

   Remember to save your memories by recording them in your Science Record Book or Calendar. (See page 4.)

Exploring—Collecting—Saving can be kept very simple. *The important thing is to enjoy.*

SUGGESTED READINGS

Dawe, Karen. *Beach Book.* New York: Workman Publishing, 1988.

George, Elly Kree. *Please Don't Step On Me.* Cherokee, North Carolina: Cherokee Publications, 1981. (Write Cherokee Publications, P.O. Box 124, Cherokee, NC 28719-0124.)

Rockwell, Anne. *First Comes Spring.* New York: Harper Collins Publishers, 1985.

Thompson, Susan L. *One More Thing Dad.* Chicago: Albert Whitman Co., 1980.

Zim, Herbert S., and Ingle, Lester. *Seashores. A Golden Nature Guide* book. Racine, Wisconsin: Western Publishing Co., 1989.

Chapter 3
Trees Are Terrific

Can you imagine our world without a single tree?
What a sad and barren place that kind of world would be.

Some people say, "Plant a tree—Save the world."
Trees are important to our world because they—

- *Give us:* beauty and shade, nuts and fruit, wood and paper, cinnamon and cocoa, coffee and maple syrup, and so much more.

- *Help our world's air.* While making their food, trees use carbon dioxide to make oxygen for people to breathe (see page 24).

IDEA

Look around your house or classroom and find all the things that come from trees. Make a list.

TYPES OF TREES

Trees are the biggest plants in the world. There are two types of trees: evergreen and deciduous (di-sid´-u-us). (Children will enjoy learning to say this wonderful word.)

Evergreen trees have needles and pinecones and drop their needle leaves slowly throughout the year. They never lose all their

needles, so they are green year round. Most **deciduous trees** turn beautiful colors and lose their leaves all at once in the fall.

Check your yard and neighborhood to see if you have both ever-green and deciduous trees. Do you have palm trees or saguaro cactus nearby? They are very interesting special trees.

PARTS OF TREES

Trees are made up of three parts: crown, trunk, and roots. Teamwork! All parts work together so that the tree can live and grow.

Trunk

The trunk is made of wood. It looks solid, but it is filled with small, strawlike "tubes." Some tubes carry minerals and water up to the leaves from the roots. Other tubes carry food (made by the leaves) down to the roots and to all parts of the tree. You might say the trunk is like a two-lane highway.

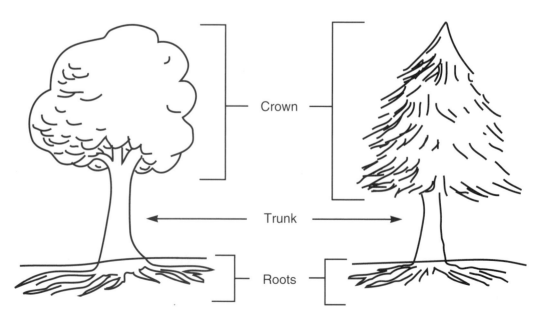

Crown

Trunk

Roots

Deciduous   **Evergreen**

IDEA

Celery Stalk Fun

Try this activity to see how the food and water travel up the tree trunk to the leaves.

How To:

1. Choose a stalk of celery with leaves.
2. Cut off the bottom edge.
3. Put the stalk in a clear drinking glass or jar with water (about half full) that has been colored with red or blue food coloring.
4. Watch and record what happens in your Science Record Book (see page 4).

   What do you think will happen? How long will it take? Does this have anything to do with how trees work? How long did you leave the celery in the glass before putting it in your compost pile (see page 160)?

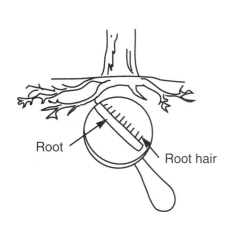

Roots

The roots have tiny root hairs growing out of the bigger roots. It is the root hairs that collect the water and minerals from the soil. The bigger roots carry these minerals and water to the trunk.

Roots usually grow out away from the trunk very close to the surface. They can reach out a distance that is equal to twice the height of the tree!

Roots keep a tree from blowing over in the wind.

Roots hold the soil in place and keep it from washing away. The washing away of soil is called **erosion** (e-row´-sion). Erosion is a big problem in our world.

IDEA

Pull Up and See

If a tiny tree that you don't want comes up in your yard, pull it out of the ground so you can look closely at the roots with your eyes and with a magnifying glass. Do you see the root hairs? Pull up a weed and an unwanted plant to see their roots.

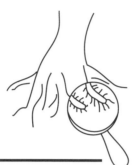

Touch the roots gently. **Smell** them to see if they have an odor. **Look** around for eroding soil. Is there any way you can keep more soil from washing away? We all need to help stop erosion.

Crown

The crown holds the leaves, which make the tree's food. The leaves are like little kitchens. Let's follow a tree's recipe for making food.

RECIPE FOR TREE FOOD

1. Tree leaves take in—
   - Sunlight
   - Carbon dioxide* from the air
2. Roots take in—
   - Food (minerals) and water from the ground
3. All of these are mixed well with the green matter in the leaf called **chlorophyll** (klor´-o-fil). This amazing

*NOTE: Carbon dioxide is a colorless, odorless, tasteless gas that is a part of our air.

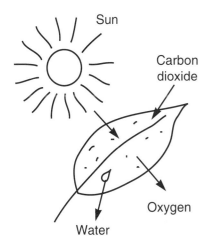

Photosynthesis

process is called **photosynthesis** (foˊ-to-sinˊ-thi-sis). It is fun to say this word.

Result: Less carbon dioxide in our air (because the leaves use carbon dioxide while making tree food) and more oxygen in our air (because the leaves give off oxygen and water as they make tree food).

Hurrah for trees! They make more oxygen for people to breathe.

IDEAS

Collect Some Tree Leaves

Look at several different kinds of tree leaves with a magnifying glass. Look underneath the leaf. What do you see? Try to find the tiny holes in the bottom side of the leaves that let in the air. *Touch* the leaf veins and see how they connect. *Look* at the veins in your hands and compare them to the veins in the leaf. Are they the same or different? How?

Leaf Rubbings

Leaf rubbings can be lots of fun. Teamwork helps. You can save your rubbings in a folder or a book made from typing paper with a construction paper cover.

How To:

1. Fat crayons work the best.
2. Remove all paper from the crayon and rub it on paper (on its side) until the crayon has a nice, flat surface.
3. Collect some pretty leaves (fresh ones—not dry) from different trees.

Continued.

4. Tape them onto cardboard or heavy paper* with the rough-vein-side up. One person can hold the leaf in place while the other one tapes.

5. Now cover the taped leaves with paper.

6. One person holds the paper and taped leaves firmly in place while the other person rubs hard with the flat side of the crayon. Take turns holding and rubbing.

You may want to use your beautiful leaf rubbings to make your own greeting cards.

HAPPY BIRTHDAY, GRAMMY!

HAPPY BIRTHDAY, THANK YOU, I ♥ YOU!

Be creative! Perhaps use more than one color.

*NOTE: Older children can hold the leaves firmly without using tape. The tape does show through but makes it easier for young children. Remember, with young children it is having fun with the process that counts and not how the product looks (see page 3).

TREES CAN TELL YOU HOW OLD THEY ARE! DO YOU KNOW HOW?

If you look at a tree stump you will discover the story of that tree. The story is told by the **rings.**

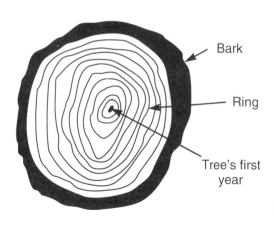

Bark

Ring

Tree's first year

How to Read the Rings

Each ring shows one year's growth. There is a light and dark part to each ring. If you count the number of rings in a tree stump, you will know how old the tree was when it was cut down.* Tree branches have rings too. Some rings are wider than others. Sunlight, water,

*NOTE: It is sometimes difficult to count the rings on a tree stump unless the cut was very clean.

> DO NOT CUT TREES DOWN UNLESS IT IS ABSOLUTELY NECESSARY. TREES ARE VERY IMPORTANT TO OUR WORLD.

and temperature make the difference. If a tree ring is wide, that year the tree probably received lots of sunlight and water and the temperature was just right for growth. A narrow ring might mean that the year was very dry and the tree grew slowly.

If you must cut down a tree, why not plant another one!

Where Can You Find a Tree Stump?

- You or your neighbor may need to cut down a tree because it is dead or too close to the house. Also, look at the rings on the branches when a tree is pruned.

- Farmers often cut and clear away trees. If you know a farmer, maybe he or she will let you go along when it is time to cut down trees.

IDEAS

1. Look at the rings on a stump and a branch of a tree. Can you tell the tree's age by counting the rings? Can you tell the years that were wet and warm? Do you see a narrow ring, which probably means the year was dry?
2. Can you count the rings from the outside toward the center of the stump until you find the year you were born—or the year of some other important event?
3. Write in your Science Record Book about your adventures with tree rings, leaves, and roots. Perhaps you will want to put in a leaf rubbing or tree-stump rubbing.

PLANT A TREE—CREATE A LIFE-LONG MEMORY

Planting a tree with a child, your family, or a group of children is an exciting and meaningful experience for all.

Planting a tree is not only fun but also—

- Provides a terrific opportunity for adult-child communication and cooperation from the planning stage throughout the whole process.
- Creates a lasting memory for each adult and child involved in the planting.
- Helps our world, since trees use carbon dioxide and give off oxygen during their food-making process (see page 25).

IDEA

Plant a Tree

Plant a tree in honor of a birthday or special occasion to make the event even more meaningful. These can be precious moments between adults and children, moments that will be remembered for a lifetime.

Before You Plant a Tree

1. Help everyone understand and appreciate how amazing and important trees are by reading together the facts and enjoying the activities suggested in this chapter, Trees Are Terrific.

2. Be sure that the child or children take part in the planning. Together think about—Where should we plant the tree? What size tree do we want when it's fully grown? How fast do we want the tree to grow? Do we want a shade tree or an ornamental tree? Could we plant a tree that will attract birds? Do we want a tree that will give fruit?

3. Next, seek advice from your state forestry department or a tree nursery. This is very important because only an expert can recommend the exact kind of tree that will do well in a certain place and also meet your needs.

4. Ask the forester or nursery person to explain exactly when and how to plant the tree and how to take care of it after it is planted.

When You Plant a Tree

1. Decide whether you want the tree planting to be a special family moment or whether you want to make a party of the occasion.

2. If you decide on a party, invite your friends, relatives, and neighbors to your "tree planting party." Let everyone help dig the hole for the new tree.

Dirt cake

3. Let all ages help plan and prepare the refreshments for the party. Perhaps serve "dirt cake" (recipe on page 190). This cake is delicious and is served from a new flower pot. Try it—it is fun! ☺

4. Take your guests on a neighborhood tour, sharing the names of trees (see page 31) and the interesting things you have found out about trees.

5. Show everyone your tree parts collection (see page 34).

After You Plant the Tree

1. Chart your tree's growth in your Science Record Book (see page 4).

TREE GROWTH CHART

DATE PLANTED
HEIGHT
DIAMETER

2. Have a "birthday" party for your tree each year.

What if You Live in an Apartment or Condominium?

- Don't let this stop you. There are several varieties of trees that grow very well in pots or planters inside. Talk with someone at a tree nursery about the kinds of trees that will match your needs.

- Some communities have parks that accept donations for memorial and special occasion trees. Perhaps a plaque could be placed on the ground at the base of the tree in honor of your child on his or her birthday or to mark some other special event. Contact your park office to arrange the details.

- Some park and recreation departments have beautification programs and special days when children and adults can help plant trees.

THE NAME GAME

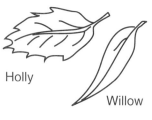

Holly

Willow

Cottonwood

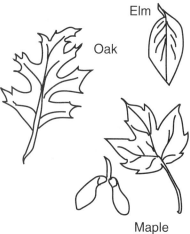

Elm

Oak

Maple

It is much more fun to call people and things by name. Have fun learning the names of trees in your yard and in your neighborhood. You can learn a tree's name by looking at its leaves and other parts.

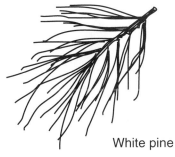

White pine

How Can You Find Out the Names of Your Trees?

First see if your tree leaves look like any of the leaf pictures on these pages.

If you need more help,

Ash

- Ask your neighbors, friends, and grandparents.

- Borrow a tree identification book from the library or buy the *Golden Nature Guide Series* book entitled *Trees* (see Helpful Resources, page 6).

- Take a small section of a tree branch with leaves to a tree nursery. They will know what kind of tree it is.

- Write to your state's department of conservation (see Helpful Resources, page 6) requesting a tree booklet.

- Visit a nearby botanical garden or arboretum where all the trees are labelled.

Tulip (tree)

IDEAS

Tour Your Yard

Take a tour of your yard and see what kinds of trees you find there. It will be fun to make a list of the trees or draw a map.

The child or children in the family can use the map to take friends or grandparents on a guided tour when they visit. Each time you plant a new tree you can update the map and put the date it was planted by the new tree's place on the map. Why not make a map for your neighborhood too!

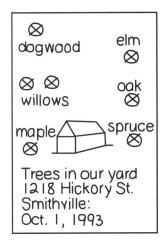

⊗ dogwood elm ⊗

⊗ ⊗ oak ⊗
willows

maple spruce
⊗ ⊗

Trees in our yard
1218 Hickory St.
Smithville:
Oct. 1, 1993

Continued.

Adopt a Tree

1. Choose a special family or class tree.
2. Learn its name.
3. Measure the tree (use a cloth tape measure) to see how big around and how tall it is—if you can reach it. Teamwork will help.
4. Mark these numbers in your Science Record Book (see Helpful Hints, page 4).
5. Look at and feel the tree's parts— bark (bumpy or smooth?), leaves (simple or compound?).

Simple   Compound

6. Check to see if any roots show above the ground.
7. Take snapshots and draw pictures of your special tree in all four seasons.

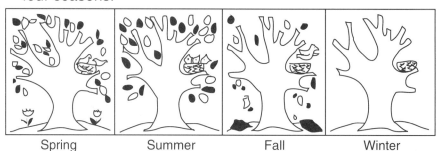

Spring   Summer   Fall   Winter

8. Watch for buds, flowers, seeds, and all changes.
9. Does your tree have flowers, acorns, fruit, or nuts?

Flowers   Acorn   Fruit   Nut

10. Does any insect or animal use it for a home?
11. Are harmful insects chewing on its leaves?
12. Do you see any galls on its leaves, branches, or trunk? (Galls are abnormal growths that form on leaves, stems, or roots of plants. They are caused by

Galls

insects, bacteria, or fungi.) They are very interesting and fun to look for. Look up the word *gall* in an insect book and in the *World Book Encyclopedia.*

13. Show off your special tree to other people.

14. What else can you find out about your tree?

 FACT Animals, birds, insects, and spiders often live in trees.

Tree Treasure Hunt

1. Read chapter 2, Exploring—Collecting—Saving.

2. Decide on the rules of the game: Where will you look for tree treasures? Only in your backyard? On your block? In the woods? How long will you look? Fifteen minutes, all day, all year?

3. Everyone becomes a detective, working together as a team, tracking down—

   - The fattest tree
   - The thinnest tree
   - The tallest tree
   - The shortest tree
   - Smooth bark
   - Bumpy bark (remember not to pick bark off of the tree)
   - All kinds of leaves
   - Leaves with worm holes
   - Trees with—
     Acorns
     Fruit

Continued.

Woodpecker holes

Insect holes

A birds nest

A squirrel nest

- A dead tree

- An evergreen with pinecones

- A tree with galls on its leaves, branches, or trunk (see Adopt a Tree, page 32, about galls).

Any other ideas for your Tree Treasure Hunt?

COLLECT TREE PARTS

Trees have many parts that are interesting to collect such as leaves, seeds, and bark.

While collecting tree parts both children and adults will have fun and learn so many interesting things about trees.

What to Collect

SEEDS

 After a tree flowers, the tree's seeds begin to form. In each seed is a baby plant that could become a new tree.

IDEAS

Dogwood

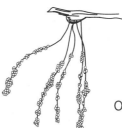

Oak tree flower

1. See if you can find flowers on trees. They usually bloom in spring, and some may look different than most flowers you see.

Apple seeds

Acorn

Pinecone

Maple tree seeds

Sweet gum ball

2. Look for seeds that come from trees. Apple tree seeds hide inside of apples. Oak tree seeds are called acorns. Evergreen seeds are in the pinecones. Maple tree seeds fall like helicopters. Gum balls from sweet gum trees have many seeds inside. When the gum ball dries out, the seeds are easy and fun to shake out.

SEEDS

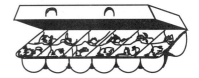

3. Collect seeds in cups or containers with lids. You may want to keep the cups in a box or sort the seeds in an egg carton.

4. See how many different kinds of evergreen trees you can find. Collect a small piece of branch with needles and a pinecone from each kind. Rub the needles between your fingers and feel the oil. Notice the special smell. Pinecones make beautiful wreaths and candle holder decorations or look nice arranged in a bowl. Sometimes ripe seeds will shake out of a pinecone just like pepper shakes out of a shaker.

LEAVES

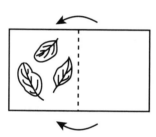

PRESSING LEAVES. It is fun to have a collection of leaves. To press leaves, place fresh leaves flat between sheets of a phone book. The next day when the leaves are flat and somewhat dry, scotch tape them onto paper. Be sure to put tape on each point of the leaf. Label the leaves and keep the sheets in a folder or scrapbook.

Sometimes pressed leaves last a long time.

WAXING LEAVES. To keep leaves a longer time, you may try waxing them. (ADULT SUPERVISION IS REQUIRED BECAUSE A WARM IRON IS USED.)

How To:

1. Fold a piece of waxed paper in half.
2. Crease it and then open it up again.
3. Place leaves on one side.
4. Fold the paper over again and iron it with a warm iron (low setting).
5. Label the sheets with masking tape or gummed strips and keep them in a folder or a scrapbook.

IDEAS

Stained Glass Surprise!

Children enjoy doing this. Try making a "sandwich" of leaves, waxed paper, and liquid starch. Besides being fun to do, this makes a lovely gift too!

You Need

1. Waxed paper: two sheets the size you want your finished "window" to be.

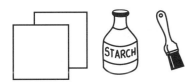

2. Liquid starch and a bowl to pour it in.

3. Small paint brush: 1- or 2-inch wide bristles.

4. Pretty fall leaves (not too dry) of different colors.

5. Rolling pin (optional).

How To:

1. Put newspapers down on the floor in an out-of-the-way place.

2. On a washable table or counter, lay one sheet of waxed paper and smooth it down flat.

3. Paint the liquid starch on generously. It will bead up and that is okay.

4. Lay your leaves on the starchy waxed paper, being sure there is a blob of starch under each leaf.

5. Dab more liquid starch on top of each leaf.

6. Cover your "sandwich" with the other sheet of waxed paper.

7. With your hands, pat and gently rub your "sandwich" so it will stick together. It is also fun to roll it gently with a rolling pin.

8. Now carefully pick up your "sandwich" with two hands and lay it flat on the newspaper to dry overnight.

9. Make sure you clean up after yourself.

10. After it dries, staple the corners to be sure it stays together. Then you may cut the edges with pinking shears for a pretty finish or make a frame with construction paper.

When you tape it up in a sunny window, *surprise—it looks like a stained glass window!*

Playdough Leaf Prints

Make leaf prints in playdough. Press a fresh leaf into rolled out playdough (see page 191) to make prints. To keep a print, roll or put the dough out in a plastic lid. Press a leaf in and let the dough harden.

Does it work better to remove the leaf right away or leave it in the dough? Why not try both ways?

BARK

Bark covers the trunk and protects the tree much like a person's skin covers and protects her or his body. It is very important to the tree. Disease and insects can enter when a tree's bark is damaged. NEVER PULL BARK OFF OF A LIVING TREE!

IDEAS

Children Love to Touch and Collect Bark

1. Look for loose bark on the ground.
2. Begin a Bark Box and collect examples of smooth, bumpy, thick, thin, curly, and flat bark.
3. Notice if bark is always the same color and thickness and if it has an odor.
4. If you are cutting down a tree or pruning trees, it is interesting to take off some fresh bark. Feel the moisture on the tree and on the back of the bark. Notice how cool it is. Does it have an odor?

Bark Rubbings

One person holds the paper flat and firmly on the tree bark while the other person rubs.* This is another way to notice different bark textures. Perhaps you will want to put your favorite bark rubbing in your Science Record Book (see page 4).

Help Children Understand Life Cycles

Knowledge gained from this chapter about trees can help children understand that the **death of a tree** is important too.

Children in today's world have little opportunity to experience and understand the complete and natural progression of life, which we call a life cycle.

*NOTE: Older children can hold the paper and do the rubbing without the help of another person.

If we can help children gain this understanding, we can also—

1. Help to lessen their fears of the unknown.

2. Help them to feel more confident about themselves.

3. Begin to prepare them for the more personal losses we all face in life.

When we were a rural society, people of all ages experienced and therefore understood the natural life cycle of plants and animals. They planted seed, which grew into plants. These plants lived their lives, produced more seeds, and then died. The dead plants were plowed back into the ground to decay and enrich the soil and provide good nourishment for the next crop of seeds. The cycle of animal life was also witnessed and understood. (See page 76 for more about animal life cycles.)

Be sure to use the new understanding about trees gained from this chapter to help children understand and see value in the death of a tree. As you talk with children about seeds growing into new trees, which grow and live their lifetimes (sometimes long and sometimes short), **be sure to talk about the last part of a tree's life—its death.**

Plants don't live forever. Every tree in the forest will someday die and fall back down to the ground. It will rot away (a term even very young children can understand) and slowly turn back into dirt. Then it will be good food for new seeds that will grow in it. You can explain that trees cut down in the city are ground up into mulch that people can take home to put into their gardens.

Take your child or children to a nearby park or forest where fallen trees are left alone to **decompose** (another great word for children). Look for fallen trees in different stages of decay. **Touch** and **smell** the rotting trees. **Look** for fungus and tiny creatures such as centipedes, millipedes, sowbugs, and termites (see page

Continued.

57) that are in the rotting log helping with the decaying process. Earthworms help too. All these important creatures are called **decomposers.**

Call your community forestry department and also nearby parks to find out what they do with the trees they cut down. Ask if you can bring some children to see the mulch pile (if they have one). Learn more about composting and start a compost pile in your yard (see page 160).

Act Out a Tree's Life Cycle

Pretend to be an acorn that a squirrel has buried under the ground. Feel the rain and warm sun—Sprout into a little oak tree and begin to grow toward the sun—Get leaves—Lose your leaves in fall—Get new leaves in spring. Years and years go by and you are now an old, old oak tree. Fall over onto the forest floor—Rot away back into the earth—Feel new little trees growing up from the wonderful soil you made when your life as a living tree was over. Then the story starts all over again.

Remember: **nature never wastes anything!**

Visit an Apple Orchard

Pick apples, brings lots home, eat lots,* and make your own applesauce (see Yummy in the Tummy, page 184). Visit your library and ask about story books involving trees and forests. How about reading *Once There Was a Tree* by Natalia Romanova and the Caldecott Medal book *A Tree Is Nice* by Janice May Udry.

*NOTE: Before eating apples right off the tree at the orchard, be sure to wash off any spray that may be on them.

SUGGESTED READINGS

Udry, Janice May. *A Tree Is Nice*. New York: Harper & Row, 1956.

Romanova, Natalia. *Once There Was a Tree*. New York: Dial Books, 1985.

Lavies, Biana. *Tree Trunk Traffic* (color photographs). New York: E. P. Dutton, 1989.

Schwartz, David. *The Hidden Life of the Forest* (color photographs). New York: Crown Publishers, Inc., 1988.

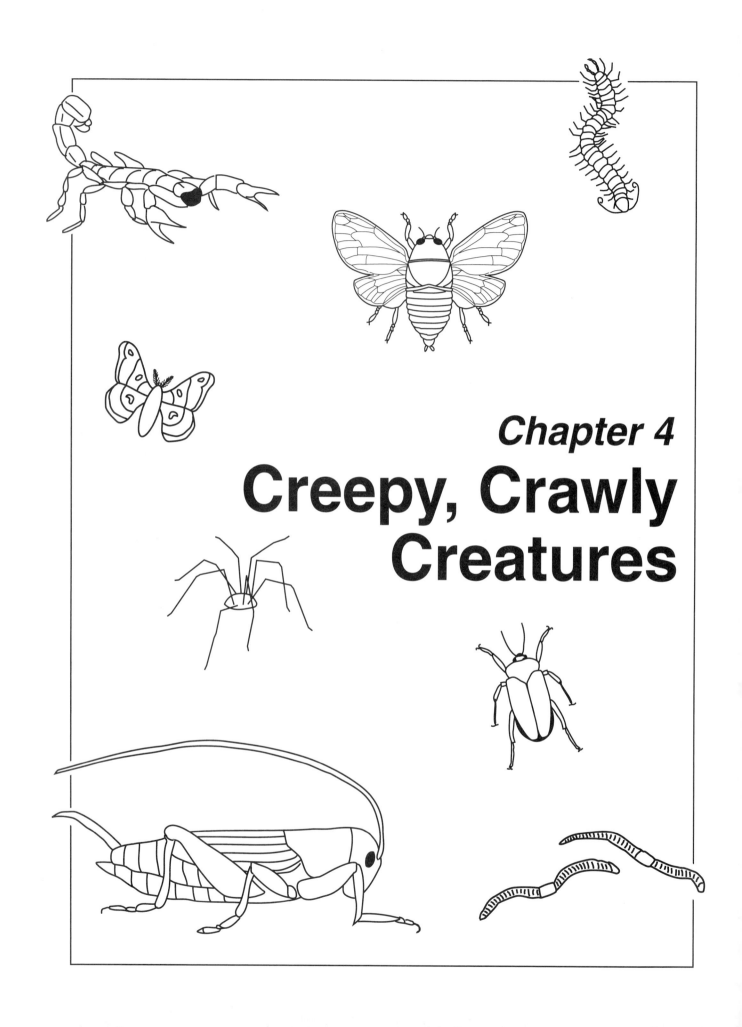

Chapter 4
Creepy, Crawly Creatures

Nature is full of creepy things
So let's enjoy the fun they bring!

Some adults carry fears and have aversions to certain creatures that they learned as young children. It is exciting to help children feel that all creatures are interesting instead of yucky! Along with a better understanding of these creatures will come new confidence and fewer unfounded fears. Even ticks and chiggers are interesting. Do you suppose they serve any worthwhile purpose?

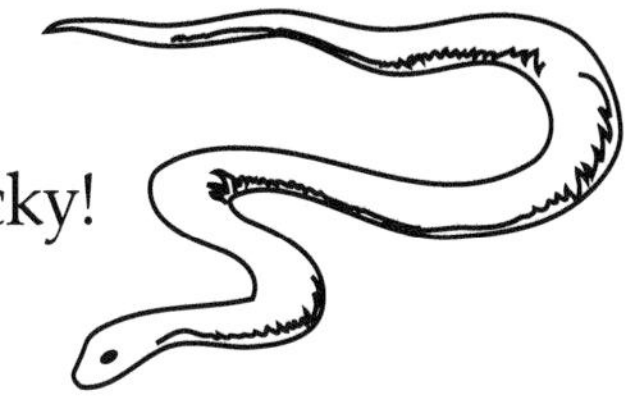

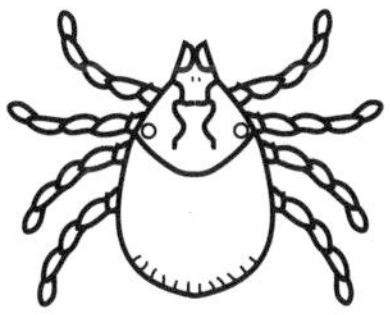

Learning the truth about creatures is *fun*. Let's begin with insects and their relatives.

INSECTS

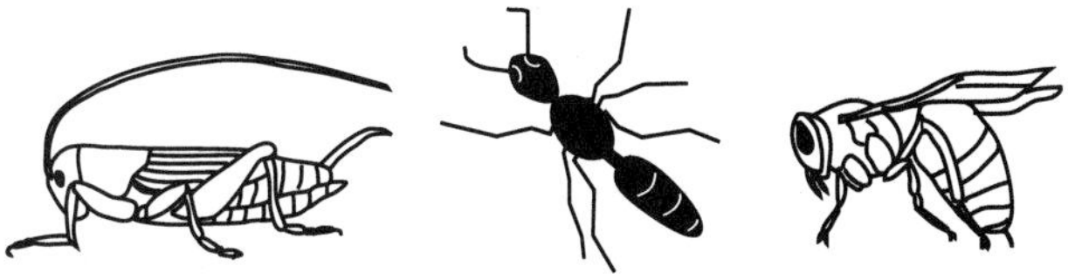

What is an insect? A fun and easy way to find out is for adults and children to make their own insects. You need a few facts and then creating begins.

FACTS

Insects usually have—

1 pair antennae (an-ten´-e) (see Facts, page 47)

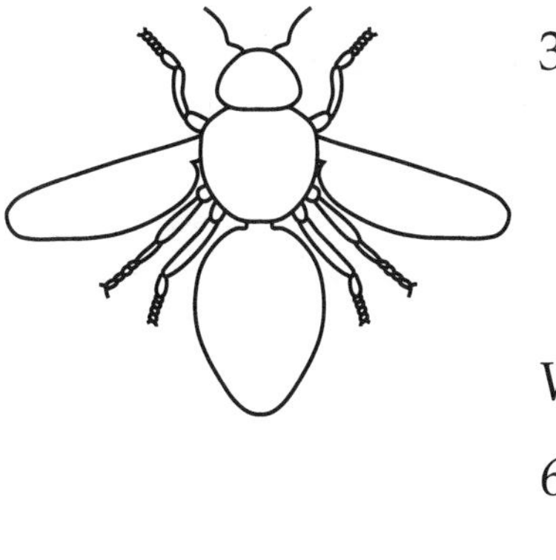

3 body parts:
    Head
    Thorax
    Abdomen

Wings—2 pair, or 1 pair, or no wings at all

6 legs (attached to the thorax)

IDEAS

Draw Your Own Insect

How To:

1. Read the facts and look at the drawing at the bottom of page 43.

2. Children and adults draw their own imaginary insects using bright colored markers or crayons and any kind of paper.

3. You may want to frame your picture by placing it on a larger piece of construction paper or cardboard you have cut from boxes or saved from packaging.

Remember: Everyone's insect will be different. There is no wrong way. Some children's insects will not have all the body parts. **The fun of doing the activity together is what counts!**

Cut and Glue or Paste Your Own Insect

NOTE: Children who can use scissors will enjoy doing all the steps described here. Even very young children can enjoy pasting or gluing on precut body parts provided by an adult or older child. (See Helpful Hints, page 3, for gluing and pasting tips.)

How To:

1. Trace the insect body part patterns found on page 45 or create your own shapes and cut them out.

2. Place the patterns on several colors of paper or on white paper. (If white paper is used, the parts may be colored later.)

3. Draw around and cut out your insect's body parts.

4. Glue or paste your body parts on colored or white paper or cardboard.

5. Draw the legs, antennae, and wings on your insect (wings optional).

6. You may wish to frame your insect picture. (See direction 3 under Draw Your Own Insect, above.)

Continued.

Patterns for Insect Body Parts

Patterns for Butterfly and Moth Body Parts (see Flannelboard Fun, page 53)

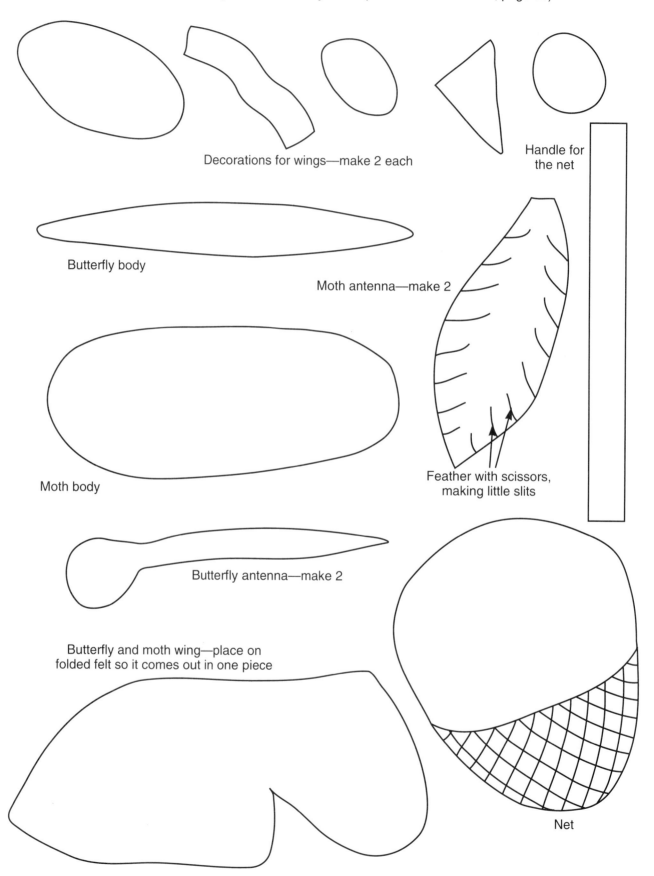

Decorations for wings—make 2 each

Handle for the net

Butterfly body

Moth antenna—make 2

Moth body

Feather with scissors, making little slits

Butterfly antenna—make 2

Butterfly and moth wing—place on folded felt so it comes out in one piece

Net

Remember: Everyone's insect will be different. There is no wrong way. Some children's insects will not have all the body parts.

Have fun doing this together.

Display Your Insect Pictures

Put them on your refrigerator or on a bulletin board. Invite your family and friends to see your creations. Serve "Ants on a Log" (See Yummy In the Tummy, page 182) for refreshments.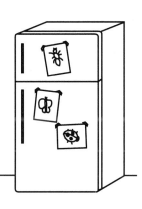

Ask everyone at the party this question, Can you think of one insect that does not have wings?

Go outside and look for some ants. Sit down and enjoy watching them. Notice how they use their antennae, how strong they are, where they are going. Ask the librarian in the children's section to help you find a book on these interesting creatures.

FACTS

- An insect's **antennae** are "feelers," and sometimes the antennae notice odors too. One feeler is called an antenna. Two are called antennae (an-ten´-e). You may also choose to say antennas, but why not use the scientists' choice, an-ten´-e?

- Insects develop in different ways. In the simplest (like the silverfish) the newly hatched insect is like a miniature adult.

More advanced insects (like the dragonfly) go from egg—to nymph—to adult. This is called **incomplete metamorphosis.**

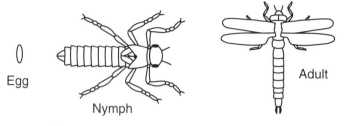

Egg   Nymph   Adult

Incomplete metamorphosis

Others (like the housefly) go through four stages as they develop: egg, larva, pupa, and adult. This is called **complete metamorphosis.** Now isn't that *amazing!*

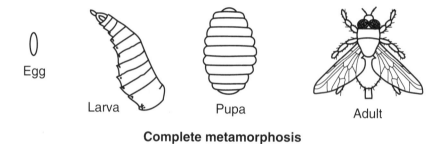

Egg   Larva   Pupa   Adult

Complete metamorphosis

 FACTS

- All insects have their skeleton on the outside of their body. It is called an **exoskeleton.**
- Insects **molt** (shed their skin) until they reach adult size. They do this because their skin doesn't stretch and as their inside body gets bigger it needs more room.

IDEAS

Collect Insects

Decide to have an insect collection! It is easy, fun and very interesting. Please do not kill insects for your collection. Once you decide to collect insects, you will notice dead ones here and

there. Collecting insects is a great way to learn about these amazing creatures.

At first children may want to collect every dead insect in sight, but they will become more selective in time.

You really do not need to worry about germs. Little hands will wash!

Collecting encourages: careful examination, sorting, and categorizing.

How To:

Keep it simple.

Here are a few helpful ideas:

- Place a small dab of liquid glue in a little box, a bottle cap, or a jar lid. Carefully place your insect in the glue.
- Place a thin layer of cotton on the bottom of the container you plan to use. This will keep the insect or insects in place.

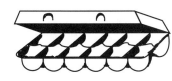

- Small jewelry boxes, margarine tubs, and boxes with clear plastic lids are great for keeping your insects. Egg cartons are helpful, too.
- Sturdy insects like the cicada (see page 50) can be speared with a floral or straight pin for easy handling. Wrap tape around the point.

Insect books will have suggestions for more involved methods of collecting and displaying.

Watch Insects

Watching live insects is also very interesting. My philosophy is to watch the insects for a short time and then set them free.

"Bug keepers" may be purchased or made easily by cutting the top out of a shoe box lid and stapling 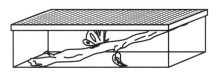 or taping nylon net in its place. The lid is then see through and it is still easy to remove. (See Caterpillar to Butterfly, page 54.)

Meet the Amazing Cicada!

Have you ever found a crunchy, light brown skeleton on the ground or stuck to a tree? In late spring and summer in parts of the country that have deciduous trees (see page 21) you will often find cicadas.

Theirs is one of the most interesting true stories in the insect world.

Look up *cicada* in an insect book or the *World Book Encyclopedia* and prepare to be amazed.

THE TRUE LIFE STORY OF CICADAS

- The female cicada lays eggs on twigs up in trees. Tiny nymphs hatch out of the eggs, fall to the ground, and bury themselves underground. They get food from the tree roots and grow bigger.

- After a certain time (see the first fact below) the nymph crawls out of the ground, climbs up, and sticks on something close by.

- The nymph splits open the skin on its back, and the adult cicada crawls out and leaves the empty skeleton behind.

- The cicada rests, pumps its wings, and then flies up into the trees.

- The nymphs of different types of cicadas stay underground different lengths of time. The ones that come out after being buried for 13 and 17 years emerge all at once. What a chorus and what a feast for birds and animals. Some cicadas come out each year.

■ Male cicadas sit in the trees and make noises to attract the female cicadas. Listen for them!

■ Cicadas do not live very long. They reproduce and then die.

IDEAS

Act Out the Cicada Story

Children love to act out the story of the cicada life cycle—pretending to be eggs up on the twigs—falling down to the ground—digging down underground—curling up tight—crawling up and out—climbing and sticking on something—crawling out of their skins—pumping their wings—deciding whether to be noisy daddy cicadas or egg-laying mothers.

Help them by telling the true story as they act it out. They love it when adults do the acting out too!

Collect Cicada Skins

Cicada skins are easy to find. Alive or dead adult cicadas are more difficult but not impossible to find. I hope you find both for your collection. (See Collecting Insects, page 48.)

Butterflies and Moths

Children love the book *The Very Hungry Caterpillar* by Eric Carle. This book is wonderful fun but not all fact.

It is fun to find out the facts and then reread the book!

FACT	Butterflies	Moths
When they fly:	Day	Night
Body shape:	Skinny	Fat
Antennae:	Straight with little knobs	Feathery
Wings' position at rest:	Pointing straight up with tips touching	Spread out to the sides
Caterpillar hatches from:	Egg laid by the female butterfly	Egg laid by the female moth
Caterpillar eats:	Leaves of the plant where the egg was laid	Leaves of the plant where the egg was laid
Emerge from:	Chrysalis	Cocoon

Now can you pick out the facts from the make-believe as you read *The Very Hungry Caterpillar*? Talk about it together and then see page 70 to find out what I think.

- Butterfly and moth wings are "decorated" in perfect **symmetry:** The two top wings are just alike, and the two bottom wings are just alike. Look at pictures to see that this is true. Try decorating your butterfly and moth pictures this way.

- The average life span of a butterfly is about 2 weeks.

- Butterflies have a long tongue, called a **proboscis** (pro-bos´-sis), which is curled up like a spring until the butterfly uncurls it into a flower to suck up the nectar.

IDEAS

A Picture Can Tell The Tale

Adults and children can tell the life cycle story of butterflies and moths by making a simple picture. It might look like this.

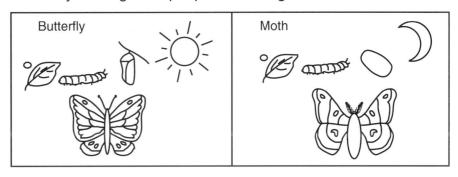

Flannelboard Fun

Cover stiff cardboard with flannel cloth to make a flannelboard. (It should be at least 18 by 22 inches.) It is a lot of fun to use the butterfly and moth felt pieces (see patterns on page 46) with the poem on page 54. This idea works well with a class of 20 children, a few children, a mix of children and adults, or one child.

How To:

1. Use colorful felt and trace the pattern pieces as directed on page 46.
2. Cut out your patterns, draw around each piece on your felt, and cut out.
3. Give at least one felt piece to each person. As you pass out the felt pieces, tell each person what the piece is. For example, "you have the moth's fat body," or "you have the butterfly's wings." Pass out all the pieces.
4. Have someone hold the flannelboard up in front of those people who are playing the game.
5. As the poem is read, each person comes up and places the piece just named in the poem on the flannelboard. When the poem is over, the felt pieces are all in place and the picture is complete.

Continued.

The person reading the poem may suggest that the people holding the wing decoration pieces "decorate" after the butterfly is in place and after the moth is in place—or after both are in place—as you wish!

Remember the symmetry fact on page 52, as you "decorate" both the moth and the butterfly.

This "game" is a perfect climax to the butterfly and moth facts and fun found on the previous pages. 😊

Butterflies and Moths

Carol Oppenheim

Butterfly, with your skinny body
Your straight antennae have little "knobies."
You fly around when the sun is high
And rest with your wings pointing straight to the sky.

Lovely moth, just as fat as can be,
Your feathery antennae are pretty to see.
You fly around when the moon is about
And rest with your wings lying straight out.

I could catch you both in my little net,
But I won't hurt you, on that you can bet.
You should both be flying as free as can be
And not in a box for people to see.

(Patterns for felt pieces to use with the poem are on page 46.)

Caterpillar to Butterfly

Watching a caterpillar change into a butterfly is fascinating and packed with fun and learning for all ages.

In spring, plant parsley, carrot, or dill plants to attract the black swallowtail butterfly. The mother butterfly lays her eggs on these plants, and the caterpillars eat this plant after they hatch. Most caterpillars will not eat substitute leaves. Milkweed plants (there are many kinds) attract the monarch butterfly. So—

1. Watch these plants closely for caterpillars.

2. Place the caterpillar and its preferred food in your Bug Keeper. Keep *fresh* food always available.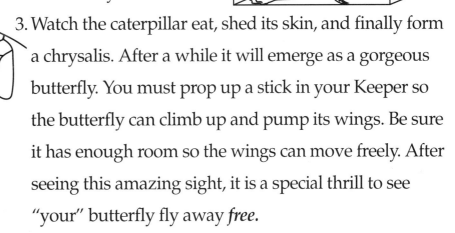

3. Watch the caterpillar eat, shed its skin, and finally form a chrysalis. After a while it will emerge as a gorgeous butterfly. You must prop up a stick in your Keeper so the butterfly can climb up and pump its wings. Be sure it has enough room so the wings can move freely. After seeing this amazing sight, it is a special thrill to see "your" butterfly fly away *free.*

4. Gather up friends and neighbors of all ages and have a Let the Butterfly Go Party.

If you can discover what food moth caterpillars eat, you can watch a moth emerge from its cocoon!

Check to see if your Department of Conservation or Natural Resources offers a booklet on butterfly gardening. Such a book will help you learn which plants will attract other butterflies or moths. Bookstores may also have such a guide.

IDEA

Act Out the Butterfly and Moth Story

Children love to act out the butterfly and moth story. They love it when an adult or older child will pretend with them.

Continued.

How To:

1. Curl up in a ball on the floor and pretend you are an egg just laid by the mother moth or butterfly.

2. Hatch out into a caterpillar (remain on the floor).

3. Nibble the kind of leaves where the mother laid your egg and become very fat. (Remember, most caterpillars will not eat substitute leaves.) Shed your skin as you grow.

4. Each person now decides if he or she will pretend to be a moth or a butterfly. Butterfly caterpillars form a chrysalis (put your hands above your head to form a triangle shape). Moth caterpillars spin a cocoon. (Do a circular spinning motion with your head and get into a small ball again.)

5. Everyone emerges with "wings" (arms) tight by your sides.

6. All stand up and slowly pump your arms downward, gradually raising and pumping them to full flying position.

7. To end the activity suggest, "Now let's all rest our wings." ("Butterflies" will rest with arms above their heads, "moths" with arms out to their sides.)

More Ideas About Insects

1. Buy the *Golden Guide Series* book called *Insects*. It is inexpensive and is a helpful reference.

2. Ask your librarian to help you find insect fact books and story books involving insects.

3. Talk with children about the fact that some insects are helpful to people and some are harmful. Children love ladybugs and like knowing that they help people by eating harmful aphids. Everyone knows that mosquitos are harmful. Exterminators sometimes have booklets about harmful insects to give to the public.

INSECT RELATIVES

When you are looking for insects, you often find sowbugs, centipedes, millipedes, and perhaps a slug or snail.

IDEA

Turn over rocks and flower pots and look among plants growing at the base of a tree to find these amazing creatures.

Remember to carefully turn the rocks and flower pots back over the way you found them. They are "home" to many crawly things.

These creatures are not true insects, but they are certainly interesting.

SOWBUGS

Sowbugs have a number of other names such as roly-poly, tickle bug, and wood louse. They are great to examine.

SNAILS AND SLUGS

Snails are fascinating, too. **Slugs** are snails without a coiled shell.

- Snails are found in all parts of the world: on land, in freshwater and saltwater, and in cold regions.
- Snails and slugs both have slimy bodies and must have moisture to live.
- If a razor blade were placed edge up in a slug's path, the slime would allow the slug to crawl over it unhurt.
- Some slugs are pests because they eat plants.

Examine a Sowbug

Pick a sowbug up gently and examine it with your eyes and a magnifying glass.

How many legs and antennae do you see?

My encyclopedia says they have five or more pairs of legs. Why do you think they curl up? Does it tickle when it walks on you? Please return it gently to its home.

Examine a Slug

Try to find a slug under a damp flower pot. Pick it up gently. It is slimy, but it won't hurt you a bit. Look for its two pairs of tentacles with eyes on the end of the longer pair. Feel the slime, which comes out of its body to lubricate its path.

Put a slug on a piece of black paper and see the design it makes with its slime. Ask a friend, "Who do you think made this design?"

Examine a Snail

Try to find a snail to watch. Is it fast or slow? If you are lucky, some day you may find an empty snail shell for your collection.

Spiders!

Spiders are *not* insects. They are arachnids.

Spiders are helpful creatures that do not deserve their fearsome reputation.

Most spider bites are harmless to people, but since the bite of a few spiders is harmful to people, CHILDREN SHOULD BE TAUGHT NEVER TO PICK UP SPIDERS.

It is interesting to watch spiders outside. It is an adult's job to kill any spiders you may find inside your house.

Spiders have—

2 body parts

8 legs

No wings or antennae

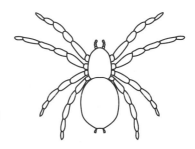

 FACTS

- Spiders belong to the arachnid family.

- Spiders catch and eat many harmful insects such as flies and mosquitos.

- Spiders paralyze their victims with a single bite from their sharp fangs. The victim is usually an insect or another spider.

- In the fangs is a "juice" that turns the victim's inside tissue into liquid, which the spider sucks into its own body for food.

Black widow

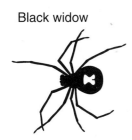

- The bite of a few spiders, such as the black widow and brown recluse, is VERY DANGEROUS to people and can cause sickness or even death.

Brown recluse

- Depending upon the kind of spider, female spiders lay anywhere from a few to 200 eggs at a time! Most spider eggs are wrapped in strong silk in an egg sac.

- Newborn spiders are tiny. Most care for themselves, but newborn wolf spiders cling to their mother's back for a week or more!

- All spiders molt and split out of their skins and leave them behind as they grow. What you think is a dead spider may be the skin. Look for spider "skins."

- All spiders make silk, but some spiders do not spin webs. Instead they hunt for food or wait for it to pass by. (Look up the trap-door spider.) See Tarantulas, page 61.

- Spider silk is so strong that some birds use it in nest building.

IDEAS

Spin a Web

It is fun to "spin a web" on a bulletin board or cardboard with yarn or string and tape or thumb tacks. Make up a web design or look in a spider book for a picture of a spider web to use as a pattern for your web. Cut out spider pictures or draw your own spiders to place in your web.

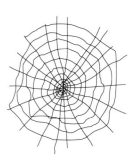

More Ideas

1. Enjoy watching spiders outside.

2. Draw your own spiders or make spiders from colored paper or egg carton sections with pipe cleaner legs—Be creative! Have fun!

3. Go on a web hunt. Watch the web daily to see what happens. Spray the web with water from a spray mist bottle and see it glisten in the sunshine. Early in the morning you may find a web with the morning dew on it. You may find a web with the sun shining through. Try taking a snapshot of a spider web. *Remember* some spiders eat their webs and may spin a new web each night. So if your web is gone, don't be too surprised.

4. Watch for a female wolf spider carrying her white egg case.

5. Ask your librarian for story and fact books about spiders. Enjoy reading *The Very Busy Spider* by Eric Carle and *Be Nice to Spiders* by Margaret Graham.

6. Find out from your state's department of natural resources or conservation about the spiders that live in your area.

TARANTULAS

Tarantulas are really helpful spiders. Their large size and shaggy look make them scary to people, but let's get the facts straight.

- Tarantulas are large, hairy, hunting spiders.
- They eat many harmful insects.
- They hunt at night and often live in abandoned lizard or rodent tunnels.
- They are shy and try to avoid people.
- Their bite would feel similar to a bee sting.
- Their bite is no more dangerous to people than the bite of other spiders.

IDEA

Look up tarantula in a spider book or in the *World Book Encyclopedia*. See if your zoo or a pet store has a live tarantula for you to see.

Spider Relatives

Chiggers, ticks, scorpions, and daddy longlegs are arachnids too. People need to know about these creatures!

CHIGGERS AND TICKS

Chiggers and ticks are not popular creatures. I cannot think of one good thing to say about them! Can you? Try to avoid getting them by using insect repellent and checking yourself for ticks *before* they begin their meal.

- Ticks bite and suck blood from humans and animals. They can carry disease.

- One female tick can lay hundreds, sometimes thousands of eggs.

- Chiggers bite people much like ticks do. They do not burrow under skin or drink blood. The chigger attaches itself to the victim's skin with special mouth parts. It injects its saliva into the skin, which dissolves the skin cells and causes the itch. It uses this liquid tissue, not blood, as food.

SCORPIONS

Scorpions are small animals with dangerous stingers on the end of their tails.

- They eat insects and spiders. The scorpion stings its victim and sucks its body juices.

- A mother scorpion's babies are born alive and ride on her back for several days.

- If a scorpion bites a person, the wound is painful but does not usually cause death.

DADDY LONGLEGS

Daddy longlegs are harmless and fun to watch. They cannot bite you. They tickle when they walk on your skin.

 Daddy longlegs are also called harvestmen.

IDEA

Look for a daddy longleg. Watch how it moves and where it goes. Will it climb up on your hand? Maybe you will see one eating an insect.

SNAKES

Let's learn about snakes. So many adults fear snakes and transmit their fear to children. If fearful adults try to understand snakes, they will find their fear easier to control.

- Most snakes are harmless and are helpful to humans.
- Snakes' food includes rats and mice. They are important in rodent control.
- Snakes do not chase people. They hope people will leave them alone.
- Snakes don't have eyelids. Their eyes are always open.
- Snakes can climb trees and are good swimmers.
- Snakes feel cool and dry—not slimy.
- Snakes' tongues are harmless and necessary in their ability to touch and smell.
- Snakes shed their skins because as they grow their skin does not. Snake skins are always inside out!

Should We Say Poisonous or Venomous Snakes?
Most people know that the bite of some snakes can cause a person to become sick or even to die. Most zoos and

many books call these dangerous snakes venomous snakes instead of poisonous snakes.

These snakes have fangs in addition to the small teeth that most snakes have.

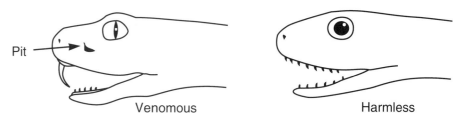

Pit

Venomous   Harmless

United States snakes

The **venom** (poisonous liquid) enters the victim through the snake's fangs when the snake bites. It is the venom and not the snake itself that is poisonous.

Venomous snakes that have a **pit** (a visible opening as seen in the picture above) are called **pit vipers.**

The picture also shows you that harmless snakes have teeth and that the eye pupil shapes are different in venomous and harmless snakes.

Children should be taught not to pick up snakes.

Since most people are not experts on snake identification, a good rule is to *leave snakes alone,* but don't forget to appreciate them as important creatures.

IDEAS

Make a Snake!

You Need:

- A discarded sock (adult size)
- Discarded panty hose or cut up rags
- Scissors—felt—glue—needle and thread.

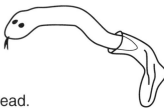

How To (the children can do most of this, but they will need some adult help):

1. Cut the legs off the panty hose.
2. Stuff them into the old sock so the "snake" is less fat at the open or "tail" end.

3. Sew up the "tail" end.

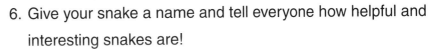

4. Cut two felt eyes and glue them on.
5. Cut a felt tongue and sew it on.
6. Give your snake a name and tell everyone how helpful and interesting snakes are!

Skin Your Snake (An adult or older child job!)

Do you want to see a snake shed its skin?

You Need:

1. The snake you just made
2. One leg cut from discarded panty hose

How To:

1. Gather up one leg from the panty hose and pull it up over your snake, beginning at the snake's tail and pulling it on so the open end is by the snake's mouth. The panty hose is the snake's "skin."
2. Gather up the open end around the nose so the skin looks "tight" but leave the tongue hanging out.
3. Pretend to rub the "skin" on a rock to loosen the skin. Now pull the "skin" back (like taking a sweater off inside out), and your snake skin will be off like a real snake leaves its skin, inside out!

More Ideas For Fun!

- Borrow library books on snakes (from the children's section) so you can learn more about snakes. *Snakes Are Hunters* by Patricia Lauber (New York: Harper Collins, 1988) is one book you may enjoy. Read about constrictors.

Continued.

- Explore with the children—What is a reptile? The *World Book Encyclopedia* will help.
- Find out about hibernation.
- Visit the zoo with your new knowledge and look for reptiles.
- When you go to the zoo, look closely at the pupils of the venomous and nonvenomous snakes. See if you can notice the pit.
- Encourage children to touch a snake in a supervised situation such as a petting zoo.
- Children love to make snakes and other creatures out of playdough. (See page 191 for a playdough recipe.) Painting dry playdough creations is fun too.
- Read and enjoy so many wonderful books about creepy crawly creatures! For some favorites see page 71.

EARTHWORMS

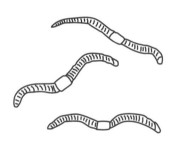

Earthworms are interesting and helpful creatures. Hold a cool, moist, wiggling earthworm in your hand. Be gentle—it can't hurt you. If you show the children that it is fun, they will probably try it too.

- Earthworms must be moist or they will die.
- They work like plows, mixing and loosening the soil.
- They don't have eyes or ears, but they can tell light from dark and feel every vibration.
- They have no bones or lungs. Oxygen passes through their skin.
- They have five pairs of hearts.

- Their **castings** (elimination) enrich the soil.

Castings

- Worms dig down deep in winter so they won't freeze.

- Earthworms are food for many other animals, such as birds, frogs and toads, and snakes. Worms make good fishing bait too.

IDEAS

Learn About Earthworms

Look up more facts about the amazing earthworm. Your library will have fact books.

Dig Up A Few Earthworms

Put the earthworms in a box with a thin layer of soil. Watch how they move. Examine them with a magnifying glass, looking for the **clitellum** (the wide band around the earthworm's body). Let them go so they won't dry out.

Clitellum

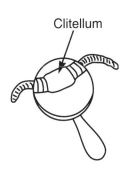

An Adventure In The Dark!

Earthworms cannot see red light. Put a piece of red cellophane over your flashlight (secure it with a rubber band) and go out to try to see night crawlers hunting for food. Even if you don't see any worms, you will have fun.

Be a Friend to Earthworms

Suggest to children that they be a friend to earthworms by moving worms trapped on sidewalks and driveways back into the grass. You will often see worms after a rain because they come up out of their wet tunnels.

Make a Home for Earthworms

Buy some night crawlers at the bait store. Examine and hold them—go fishing—and save a few to watch in a jar.

Continued.

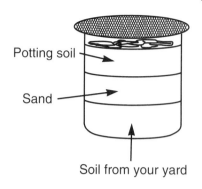

Potting soil

Sand

Soil from your yard

How To:

1. In a jar (28 oz or larger peanut butter jar will do) put in layers as shown. The material must be moist but not soggy.
2. Place 3 or 4 night crawlers on top of the top layer. The worms will tunnel down.
3. Place a thin layer of decaying leaves on top.
4. Cover the jar with nylon net, if you wish, but they won't crawl out.
5. Place a box over the jar to keep it dark. Making a "sleeve" of black construction paper or pulling a black sock over the jar works, too.
6. Check for tunnels, and in a few days **let them go.**

NOTE: It is fun to keep the worms in your jar from late fall to early spring. You must keep them moist but not soggy, so add a little water to the soil when needed. Put a few bread crumbs and a small piece of lettuce on top of the soil each week for their food. Let the children dump out (gently) the soil and worms onto a paper plate to touch them and see how they are doing. Help the children remember to be gentle and careful with the worms and to put them back in the jar before they dry out. In spring have a Let the Earthworms Go Party. Put the soil and worms into your garden. The worms and your garden will be happy.

Compost With Earthworms in Your Home or Classroom*

This activity is exciting, fun, filled with hands-on learning experience, and demonstrates before your eyes how composting works. When you have a worm compost box, you will feed your worms, count your worms, find thread-size baby worms, and even see worm cocoons with babies coming out before your eyes!

You will also have lots of visitors coming in to see how the worms are doing. I recommend you try it.

Worm cocoon

*This idea came from a wonderful book, *Two Minutes a Day for a Greener Planet,* by Marjorie Lamb (New York: Harper & Row, 1990). She calls it vermicomposting.

You Need:

- A bin with a lid—ours is in a plastic box, 9 inches high by 13 1/2 inches wide by 9 inches deep. A foam cooler or sturdy cardboard box with a plastic liner will also work.

- Set your bin on blocks, bricks, or margarine tubs with a tray, old cookie tin, or plastic lined box lid underneath.

- A drill to make about 10 small holes in the bottom of the bin for drainage.

- Some organic bedding material such as grass, straw, shredded leaves or shredded paper. We began with shredded leaves and shredded newspaper. This material should be as damp as a wrung out sponge.

- Earthworms—preferably red worms or "red wigglers" (not night crawlers). These worms are available where fishing bait is sold. We started with 100 red worms. Marjorie Lamb's chapter on vermicomposting says, "A bin of about 3 cubic feet can take up to a pound of worms."

How To:

1. Prepare your bin as described above.

2. Feed your worms the same kind of food scraps as mentioned on page 160 under composting. Be sure to cut up such things as banana peels in small pieces.

3. Dig your scraps into your bedding material. (It is hard for me to tell you how much food waste to add.) I add at least a 16 oz carton full of kitchen scraps, including some coffee grounds, each week, plus dead leaves from our house plants. Marjorie Lamb says that red worms eat their own weight in bedding every day!

4. Keep your worms away from extreme temperatures. They should be alright in a temperature range between 40 to 80 degrees Fahrenheit or 5 to 27 degrees centigrade. Have a thermometer next to your bin so the children can check the temperature.

Continued.

5. Keep your bedding material damp but not soggy. Don't worry about your worms' escaping. They like it in their dark, damp home. (The first day I did find a few worms on the tray. Perhaps they climbed through the holes. They died quickly because of lack of moisture.)

 We emptied our worm composting bin into the school's flower garden in spring. Each child had a turn to put some worms and compost material into the ground. The worms and the flowers are happy!

Are you ready to try this great worm adventure?!

 Sing "The Earthworm Song"*

(Tune—*Twinkle, Twinkle Little Star*)

Wiggling earthworms are underground,

Hiding so they won't be found.

Tunneling, tunneling is all they do.

Helping me and helping you.

Keeping our earth soft and good,

I would help them if I could.

*It is fun to let the children be your echo. You sing a line, and they echo the line until the song is finished. After they know it, you can sing it together.

ANSWERS TO "FIND OUT WHAT I THINK" ON PAGE 52

The egg hatches into a caterpillar: Fact.

The caterpillar eats many foods: Fiction.

The caterpillar spins a cocoon: Fact.

A butterfly emerges from the cocoon: Fiction.

Remember that a butterfly emerges from a chrysalis, and a moth emerges from a cocoon.

SUGGESTED READINGS

Brinckloe, Julie. *Fireflies.* New York: Macmillan Publishing Co., 1985.

Carle, Eric. *The Grouchy Ladybug.* New York: Thomas Y. Crowell, 1977.

Carle, Eric. *The Very Busy Spider.* New York: Philomel Books, 1984.

Carle, Eric. *The Very Hungry Caterpillar.* New York: Philomel Books, 1969.

George, Elly Kree. *Please Don't Step On Me.* Cherokee, North Carolina: Cherokee Publications, 1981. (Write Cherokee Publications, P.O. Box 124, Cherokee, NC 28719-0124.)

Graham, Margaret Bloy. *Be Nice to Spiders.* New York: Harper & Row, 1967.

Lauber, Patricia. *Snakes Are Hunters.* New York: Harper Collins, 1988.

McDonald, Megan. *Is This a House for Hermit Crab?* New York: Franklin Watts, Inc., 1990.

Parker, Nancy Winslow, and Joan Richards Wright. *Bugs.* New York: Greenwillow Books, 1987.

Chapter 5
Wild Creatures Great and Small

So many amazing creatures,
Some large and some so small.
Don't you think it would be fun
To learn about them all?

People of all ages are curious about wild creatures. Before you have fun finding out more about wild animals, here are some FACTS *everyone should know:*

- When you walk in the woods, you may not see any animals because many wild animals are **nocturnal** (active at night) creatures and because wild animals do not want to be near people.

- *Wild animals do not make good pets.* People should not try to keep a wild creature.

- If a person cares for a young wild creature for awhile, it loses the ability to ever take care of itself in the wild. Call a wildlife rescue organization if you find an injured wild animal.

- Baby animals are rarely abandoned. Chances are the parent is nearby.

- Park officials say that when people feed wild animals, it really kills them because—

  - Junk food is not good for them and disturbs their natural feeding habits.
  - Young animals starve because they don't learn how to find natural food.
  - Wild animals that become used to humans lose their natural wariness and become easier for predators to kill.
  - Some animals are killed by cars as they come to beg.

Feeding wildlife is against the law in many places. So respect their wildness and KEEP YOUR DISTANCE, FOR THEIR SAFETY AND YOURS. (You may be bitten by the animal and then would need to have rabies shots.)

WHAT ABOUT WOLVES?

When young children are asked, "What animals do you think live in the woods?" they often name wolves first! Do you think this might be because they fear them?

Fears often begin because of incorrect information. Children gain confidence by knowing facts.

- The wolf population in America has declined.

- Many wolves were hunted and killed by people.

- Wolves need large areas to roam, and this habitat is no longer widely available. A creature's **habitat** must include everything it needs to live—the proper food, water, shelter, space, and climate.

- In the United States (except in Alaska) wolves are an endangered species, and it is now illegal to harm them in any way.

- People *do not* have to fear being attacked by wolves. They eat mostly large-hoofed animals such as moose and deer and some small prey. (See Predator and Prey, page 76.)

Do you know if wolves still live in your state?

IDEAS

- Check with your state's department of conservation or natural resources to find out if you have wolves, foxes, or coyotes in your state. Ask a ranger or agent for information about these animals.

- Reread the old favorites *Little Red Riding Hood* and *The Three Little Pigs.* Be sure the children understand that these stories are make-believe and that real wolves are not like the ones in these stories. Once children understand the facts about real wolves, they can delight in these make-believe stories without fear. (Also see Predator and Prey, page 76).

LITTLE RED RIDING HOOD

THE THREE LITTLE PIGS

- Ask your librarian about the book *Wild, Wild Wolves* by Joyce Milton (New York: Random House, 1992). It presents wolf facts and illustrations in an appealing story.

Introduce Music Too

Children enjoy *Peter and the Wolf* by Sergey Prokofiev and *Carnival of the Animals* by Camille Saint-Saëns.

Children love to perform the following musical plays (curriculum suggestions are also included): *Three Piggy Opera* and *Three Nanny Goats Gruff* by Carol Kaplan and Sandi Becker and *The Little Red Hen* by Carol Kaplan.

A Guessing Game

Adults and children try to name all the creatures (large and small) that live in the woods in their state. Your state's department of conservation or natural resources may have wonderful free information to help you with this

Continued.

game. (See Helpful Resources, page 6). If they can't help you, the children's section of your library can provide books about such animals as raccoons, deer, skunks, porcupines, and beavers. It is fun to learn about these amazing wild animals.

PREDATOR AND PREY—A PART OF NATURE'S PLAN

Children enjoy knowing how nature's plan works! Even young children can understand that nature's plan provides food for all creatures.

IDEAS

Help Children Learn About Predators and Prey

Young children can understand that some creatures are meat eaters—they are the **predators**—and that some creatures are going to be eaten—they are the **prey**—and that sometimes predators become prey when they are eaten by other predators! Is this information frightening or reassuring to children? ***Children feel less fearful when they understand how nature's plan works.*** So how do you begin?

Explain to children that—

- Nature provides creatures with food.
- In nature's plan the very old or sick prey, such as a bunny or squirrel, whose life is almost over, will sometimes be caught by a meat-eating predator to use as its food.
- The predator is ***not mean***—it is ***hungry***. It is a meat eater and must have this kind of food.
- The young bunny, or other prey, who is healthy, strong, and quick will run away and be able to grow up and have its own babies later in its life.
- Nature produces many extra animals such as earthworms and frogs, so many other creatures will have food.
- People are predators when they fish and hunt.

 - People do not get eaten by anyone.

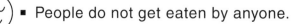

Look for Predators and Prey in Your Own Yard

Did you know that some insects like the ladybug, praying mantis, and dragonfly are helpful predators? They eat many harmful prey like aphids, flies, and mosquitos.

It is fun to see nature's plan at work. You will notice that **nature's food plan** is really a **food chain,** which always begins with the sun. Without the sun no plants or animals could live on our planet Earth. Here is a food chain—

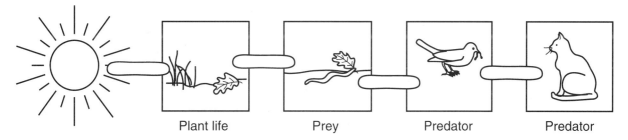

| Plant life | Prey | Predator | Predator |

In this food chain the **sun** makes the grass and leaves grow. The **earthworm** eats the grass and leaves. The **bird** eats the worm. The **cat** eats the bird! The cat does not get eaten—so that is the end of this food chain.

Playing nature's "food chain game" is fun and also helps children see that **all** plants and animals need each other and are important in our world.

Here are a few more food chains—

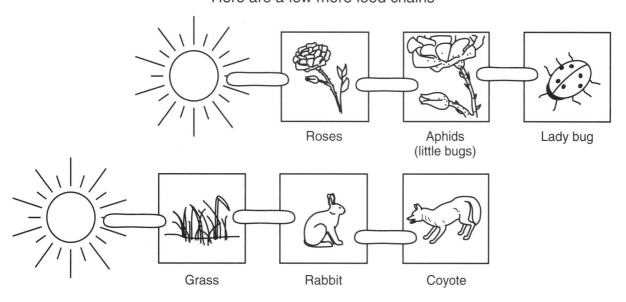

| Roses | Aphids (little bugs) | Lady bug |

| Grass | Rabbit | Coyote |

Continued.

Remember: The coyote is not mean—just hungry. The rabbit it eats will probably be old, weak, or sick.

See if you can think of more food chains. Draw pictures of the creatures in your food chains or look for animal pictures or animal stickers to use. See Birds of Prey on page 84 to find out about owls, hawks, and vultures. They are important and often misunderstood predators.

WHAT ABOUT BIRDS?

Birds give us beauty, musical songs, and insect control. Can you imagine our world without birds?

- Birds are perfectly designed for flight.
- Their feathers overlap like shingles and provide protection, "climate control," and camouflage.

Shaft

Contour feather

- A bird's feathers are strong and lightweight. Stiff contour feathers are found on the bird's body, wings, and tail.
- Down feathers are fluffier and softer and lie close to the bird's body under the contour feathers. They keep the bird warm.
- Birds don't have feeling in their feet, so don't worry that they might have cold feet.
- Birds have large eyes that can see near and faraway. They cannot roll their eyes, so they turn their heads to see in different directions. Their keen eyesight helps them find food, a mate, and a place to live.

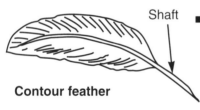

- You cannot see a bird's ears. Their ears are small holes covered with feathers located just below and in back of the eyes on each side of their head. Birds hear very well, especially the owl (see page 85).

- Birds have beaks and tongues but no teeth. A bird's **gizzard** (a special part of the stomach) grinds up the bird's food. See page 81 for more about beaks and feet.

- Birds build a nest to have a place to lay eggs and raise their young. All birds lay eggs, and most sit on their eggs (**incubate**) until they hatch and then take care of their young. Because of instinct birds build just one kind of nest and sing only certain songs. Birds cannot make choices. People are able to make many choices. **Instinct** is a behavior that seems to be already known at birth rather than learned later.

IDEAS

- Have fun finding out about one bird that does not sit on its eggs or care for its young. Look up the cowbird in a bird book or the *World Book Encyclopedia*.
- Read the delightful book *Horton Hatches the Egg* by Dr. Seuss. Does Mazie remind you of a cowbird?
- Buy a bird identification book so you can begin to know birds by name. The *Golden Nature Guide* book called *Birds* is an inexpensive basic book that is good for beginners. It is available at most book stores. Many other bird books are also

Continued.

available. Also ask friends and neighbors to help you identify birds.

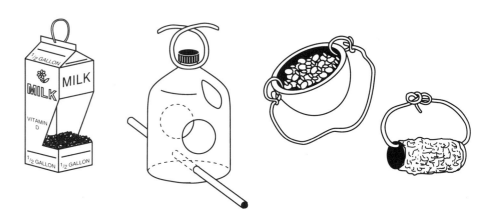

Make Your Own Bird Feeders (Adult help needed; let the children do as much as possible.)

Feeding birds allows you to see them up close. *Owning a bird identification book is necessary for maximum fun and learning.* Household throw aways can be used to make these feeders.

You Need:

1. Paper milk carton or plastic milk jug
2. Twig for the perch
3. String for hanging
4. Toilet paper roll
5. Orange or grapefruit halves
6. Food—birdseed, smooth peanut butter, raisins, cranberries

How To:

1. Look at the bird feeder pictures to see how to make the milk carton and milk jug feeders.
2. Smear the toilet paper roll with smooth peanut butter; roll it in birdseed; put a string through the roll; tie the ends of the string together.

3. Eat the orange or grapefruit; tie on the string as shown in the picture; fill with birdseed mixed with other treats such as raisins and cranberries.

4. Hang these feeders near a window so you can get a good look at your neighborhood birds.

Feeders placed in or near bushes are especially popular with birds.

Hints:

1. Ask your natural resources or conservation department for bird-feeding tips.

2. We buy mostly black oil–type sunflower seeds, some mixed seed, and niger (thistle) seeds (to attract finches).

3. Hummingbird feeders are not expensive and always have bright red parts. (Hummingbirds are attracted to red.) You can mix your own sugar water—4 parts water to 1 part sugar. You do not need to color the water red. Store it in a glass jar in your refrigerator. Wash the feeder and replace with fresh sugar water every day or so. Never use honey.

4. Woodpeckers love suet, which is fat meat. Get some from your butcher. Place it in a mesh onion bag, tie it shut, and tie it to a tree. If you have squirrels in your neighborhood, you will need to buy a sturdy suet feeder where bird-feeding supplies are sold. We tie ours on the tree with picture wire so the squirrel can't get it down.

 Good luck in keeping squirrels out of your feeders.

Fun with Beaks and Feet

As you begin to look closely at birds, be sure to notice their beaks and feet. Birds use their beaks to help them eat their own special kind of food.

Continued.

Birds use their feet in many different ways. Some birds are climbers; others are graspers, perchers, runners, or swimmers. Don't you agree that birds are amazing creatures?

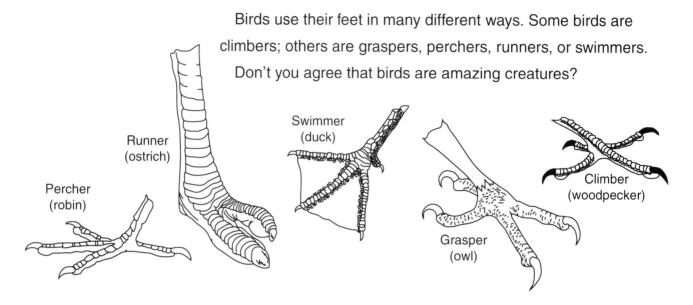

Percher
(robin)

Runner
(ostrich)

Swimmer
(duck)

Grasper
(owl)

Climber
(woodpecker)

Examine Feathers, Nests, and Bird Eggs

 As a new bird feather grows in, the old one falls out—much the same as we lose hair. I have never had a problem with germs from examining single feathers. However, WARN CHILDREN NOT TO HANDLE DEAD OR SICK BIRDS BECAUSE OF THE POSSIBILITY OF DISEASE. If possible, help children bury dead birds. A dead bird will fertilize the soil as it decomposes. (See The Importance of Life Cycles, page 38).

Feathers

Single feathers are often found on the ground. When you find a single bird feather, examine it and try to guess which kind of bird lost it. It is easy to mount a feather on an index card. (A piece of tape will hold it in place.)

Nests and Eggs

Sometimes people find a bird's nest, broken egg shells, and even a whole bird egg on the ground. If you find an unbroken egg, place it back in the nest if the nest is easy to reach. Never take a bird's nest from a tree because some birds use the same nest more than once and also because it is against the law.

BE AWARE: In the United States it is illegal to collect nests, feathers, and bird eggs found in the wild. The law allows for prosecution of people who kill birds to collect their feathers or collect nests or eggs.

WHAT ABOUT ENDANGERED ANIMALS?

Some scientists are worried that many wild creatures are disappearing because of the removal of rain forests and large areas of woods in the United States. Become aware and care.

IDEA

Animals in Trouble

It is important to help children understand that birds and other wild creatures are precious and important and that they face survival problems in our world.

How To:

1. Talk with children about how special and important birds and other wild creatures are.
2. Show concern when you hear about oil spills or cutting down of forests or water pollution that destroys the homes (habitat) of these creatures.
3. Explain to children that an animal or plant can become an ***endangered species*** if its habitat is destroyed or changed in a way that makes living and reproducing difficult. If an animal or plant dies out completely, it is then **extinct.**
4. Keep a special folder of pictures and articles from magazines and newspapers about birds and other animals that are having trouble surviving because of problems people cause.

Continued.

5. Listen and watch for this kind of news on television and radio. Tell children about this news so they will know you think it is important.

6. Explain to children what it means to become extinct. When they begin to understand food chains, see page 77, they will see that each creature is important in nature's plan.

Even very young children can understand and care about birds and all creatures.

BIRDS OF PREY

- Raptors are meat-eating birds that feed on smaller animals, including insects, spiders, fish, reptiles, other birds, and mammals.

- Raptors are predators (see Predator and Prey, page 76). By hunting and catching prey (such as rats and mice) they keep the population of these and other animals from getting too large. They feed on weak and unhealthy animals.

- Raptors have good eyesight, hooked beaks for tearing flesh, strong grasping feet with large, sharp **talons** (claws) for killing and holding prey. Only the vultures have weak feet.

- Vultures and condors are nature's "cleanup crew." They eat dead animals (**carrion**).

- Owls hunt for prey at night while the other raptors are resting.

Learn More About Birds of Prey

Eagles, hawks, falcons, vultures, and owls are called **raptors** or **birds of prey.** They are fascinating, important, and often misunderstood birds. ***All raptors are protected by state and federal laws. It is illegal to harm them or to keep them in captivity without special permits.***

WHAT ABOUT OWLS?

Some people fear owls; some people think owls are wise. Scientists have studied owls and have found out that owls are not really wise but that they are helpful not harmful to people.

- Why do owls fly at night? Because mice, rats, and other small animals they hunt are active at night.
- How do owls see? Owls' huge eyes gather lots of light so they have excellent night vision. Owls cannot move their eyes in their sockets, but they can turn their heads quickly and nearly all the way around.
- How do owls hear? Notice where the ear openings are in the picture to the left. These openings are covered by downy feathers. The right ear opening is higher than the left so they can hear sounds from high and low. Owls have excellent hearing. A barn owl can locate prey in total darkness by hearing alone.

Ear openings

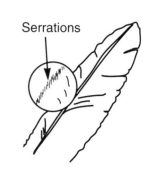

Serrations

- Can owls fly without making a sound? Yes! Their flight feathers have special edges, as you can see in this picture, so their prey cannot hear the owls coming.

- What are owl pellets? Owls swallow small prey whole and tear larger prey apart with their beaks. Hours later indigestible bones, fur, and feathers are coughed up and spit out. These firm pellets may be 1 to 2 inches long. The pellets can be broken apart and studied to learn exactly what the owl has eaten. Studies show owls eat huge numbers of rats and mice.

IDEAS

- Read *Owl Moon* by Jane Yolen (New York: Philomel Books, 1987).
- Learn all you can about owls and all the amazing raptors in our world.

Let's Pretend to Be Owls

Children enjoy pretending that it is a dark night and they are hungry owls sitting up in a tree listening and looking for a mouse to eat. The trick is to read the facts about owls, to look carefully at the owl pictures, and then to do what owls do.

The hungry owl—

- Looks down, turning its head from side to side (remember your eyes must stare straight ahead).
- Listens by cocking its head to use its special ears that can hear high and low sounds.
- Turns its head all the way around to see behind its back. People can't really do that, but try your best.

- Flies down with silent wings (arms flapping).
- Grabs the mouse with its sharp talons (pretend your feet are the talons and pounce down on the mouse).
- Flies back up to the tree limb with the mouse.
- Gobbles the mouse down in one gulp (or tears the mouse up with its beak to feed the baby owls).
- Digests the mouse—yum, yum—and finally
- Spits up the owl pellet.

Are you glad you are a person and not an owl?

WHAT ABOUT BATS?

Bats are misunderstood and feared by many people. They are truly amazing creatures.

Bats are the only mammals that can really fly! (Flying squirrels just glide.) People are mammals too. **Mammals** are warm-blooded animals that are born alive, drink their mother's milk, breathe air, and have hair and backbones. In fact, bat and human skeletons look very much alike.

Please do not believe that bats are creepy or vicious or dirty or that they get into your hair or that all bats have rabies.

Recent scientific studies show that bats are gentle, keep themselves very clean, are intelligent enough to be easily trained, and rarely give anyone rabies.

Bats can get rabies, just as dogs, cats, skunks, and other animals can, but the studies show that only a small number of bats get rabies. Those bats that are rabid rarely become aggressive. Remember this rule—If you see a sick or injured bat or any other wild animal, DON'T TRY TO GET CLOSE TO IT OR TRY TO PICK IT UP. Call a wildlife rescue organization so they can help the animal.

- There are about 900 kinds of bats in the world. The smallest weighs about as much as a penny, and the largest weighs 2 pounds and has a 6-foot wing span.
-  Bats hang upside down.
- Bats feed at night and are important in insect control. The endangered gray bat may eat 3,000 insects each night!
- Bats can see quite well but usually find their food by sending out high squeaking sounds (usually too high for us to hear) that bounce off the insect and back to the bat's ears. By using this **echolocation,** bats can catch fast-flying insects and avoid running into wires, trees, or other objects.
- Most female bats have only one baby a year. The young suck milk from their mother. Most bats live close together in nursery groups.
- Natural enemies of bats include owls. People cause problems for bats by closing cave entrances and by disturbing them in their caves. Many bats live or at least hibernate in caves. An animal that **hibernates** spends the winter in a sleeplike, inactive state.

- Some bats are endangered species. In many places all bats are protected by law.

- Fruit-eating bats are important because they spread seeds from place to place, and nectar-eating bats pollinate trees and plants.

- Bat **guano** (feces) is valuable fertilizer. Many cave creatures depend on the guano as their food.

- Bats that stay in cold places through the winter must hibernate. They store up fat and energy before their long "sleep." *Do not disturb bats.*

- Yes, there are vampire bats. They *do not* suck people's blood! They make up a very small percentage of all bats, and all live in South America. Vampire bats are a bother to South American cattle owners because they cause cows and horses to bleed and then lick the animals' blood.

Now—don't you agree that *bats are truly amazing and important animals?*

IDEAS

- Find out more about bats, including the vampire bat. Your library will have interesting books about bats in the children's section. The *World Book Encyclopedia* will help, too.
  - Find out which bats live in your state. Your state conservation or natural resources department may have helpful information to give you.
  - See if your library has any fiction books about bats. *Wufu: The Story of a Little Brown Bat* by Bernice Freschet is the only one I have found that I like.

Continued.

See Bats in Action

The best time to see bats is at dusk, which is between sunset and darkness. Go to a place where there are lots of insects. Bats are often seen chasing insects around electric lights or flying over a pond, lake, or stream.

Sit or stand quietly and watch the bats dart here and there catching their food.

Hurrah for bats!

SUGGESTED READINGS

Barlowe, D., and Barlowe, S. *Who Lives Here?* New York: Random House, 1978.

Carle, Eric. *Brown Bear, Brown Bear, What Do You See?* A Bill Martin, Jr. book. New York: Holt, Rinehart, and Winston, 1967.

Carle, Eric. *Polar Bear, Polar Bear, What Do You Hear?* A Bill Martin, Jr. book. New York: Henry Holt and Company, 1991.

Dr. Seuss. *Horton Hatches the Egg.* New York: Random House, 1940.

Dr. Seuss. *Yertle the Turtle and Other Stories* (including *Gertrude McFuzz*). New York: Random House, 1950.

Eastman, P. D. *The Best Nest.* New York: Random House, 1968.

Freschet, Bernice. *Wufu: The Story of a Little Brown Bat.* New York: G. P. Putnam's Sons, 1975.

Kaplan, Carol. *The Little Red Hen.* St. Louis: Milliken Publishing Company, 1991.

Kaplan, Carol, and Becker, Sandi. *Three Nanny Goats Gruff.* St. Louis: Milliken Publishing Company, 1987.

Kaplan, Carol, and Becker, Sandi. *Three Piggy Opera.* St. Louis: Milliken Publishing Company, 1988.

McCloskey, Robert. *Make Way for Ducklings.* New York: Viking Press, 1969.

Slobodkina, Esphyr. *Caps for Sale.* W. R. Scott, 1947.

Yolen, Jane. *Owl Moon.* New York: Philomel Books, 1987.

Morning Glory Seeds

TOMATO SEEDS

Chapter 6
Window Sill Gardening

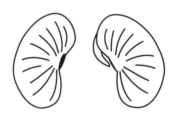

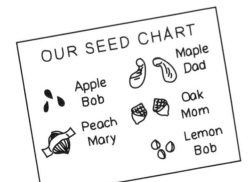

OUR SEED CHART

Apple Bob

Maple Dad

Peach Mary

Oak Mom

Lemon Bob

A magic place it seems to be,
A window sill garden for all to see.
More dear to a child than you can know,
So plant, water, wait, and watch it grow.

Children love to plant seeds and watch them grow.

From to What a thrill!

IDEA

Plant a Window Sill Garden

Let the children feel the soil and sand and do the planting and watering!

You Need:

1. A small bag of potting soil.
2. Some sand (or vermiculite from the garden or hardware store)
3. 10 oz clear plastic glasses. It is fun to see the roots.
4. An old dishpan or kitty litter container.
5. An old cloth to spread on the floor.
6. Masking tape and a permanent marker for labeling.
7. Flower pots or other containers (if you wish to transplant) See Transplanting Fun, page 98.

How To (the children take turns planting while an adult watches and helps if needed):

1. Decide which seeds to plant. (See What to Plant, page 94.)
2. Label the glass with a strip of masking tape.

| Bob's lima beans Oct. 20, 1993 |

(Child's name, seed's name)
(Day planted)

Continued.

For added interest count and record on the tape the number of seeds planted so you can see later if they all came up.

3. Spread the cloth and position the dishpan, soil, and sand (or vermiculite) in the center. (You can put the soil and sand in bowls inside the dishpan to avoid most spills.)

4. The child can then—

- Mix 3 handsful of soil and 2 handsful of sand together in the dishpan. (Talk about whether it feels smooth, bumpy, dry, wet.)
- Fill the glass about 2/3 full of the soil-sand mixture.
- Place several seeds on top of the soil (leave space between the seeds).
- Cover the seeds with more soil—about 1/2 inch.
- Add just enough water to make the soil damp. (Explain that too much water is not good for the baby plant.)
- Place the glass on a sunny window sill and watch and wait.

NOTE: An adult will need to help the children decide how often and how much water to add to keep the soil damp.

WHAT TO PLANT

Corn

Indian *corn* is a quick grower and fun. Help the children pull some kernels off of this decorative corn and plant them. ***Do not soak*** the corn before planting it. Popcorn will also grow. Also try Watch Seeds Grow, page 101, with corn seeds.

Orange, Lemon, or Grapefruit Seeds

Encourage the children to save seeds from these citrus fruits. Choose plump seeds. Soak the seeds 24 hours before planting. These seeds take longer to come up than the Indian corn but make beautiful plants. If you transplant them, you may someday have citrus trees.

Lentils

Lentils are quick and fun to grow. Buy a bag of dried lentils at the grocery store. Enjoy touching and examining these unusual seeds. ***Do not soak*** the lentils before planting. These seeds should sprout in a few days. They make a pretty plant with grey-green leaves. (See More Window Sill Fun, page 100, for more fun with lentils.)

Lima Beans

Lima beans purchased in the dried bean section of the grocery store used to be very easy to grow. Recently these seeds often rot under the soil before they sprout. What has changed? What have they done to the seeds? I wonder. Anyway, I would buy a package of the largest size dried lima beans at the grocery store and give it a try. Also buy a package of lima bean seeds anywhere that sells packaged garden seeds. These seeds are sure to grow and will even produce more lima beans if you transplant them into a bigger pot. (See Transplanting Fun, page 98.) Why not plant both grocery store and packaged garden lima bean seeds and compare the results. For more fun with limas, see Bean Soup, page

188; Watch It Grow, page 101; and Find That Baby Plant, page 99.

Packaged Garden Seeds

Buy a few packages of flower and vegetable seeds in spring and save them to plant in winter. (Unsold packaged garden seeds are picked up by many seed companies in early July, so don't wait too long to buy them.) Experiment with different seeds in your window sill garden. One year we had beautiful morning glories blooming in our window when it was wintry weather outside. What a treat!

Watermelon, Cantaloupe, Pumpkin Seeds

These seeds should sprout for you, but they will get spindly very quickly since they are vines that lie on the ground. Maybe you can transplant them in some of the containers suggested in Transplanting Fun, page 98.

Apple, Peach and Grape Seeds

I have read that these seeds need to be refrigerated for 3 months before they will grow.

Why not try this experiment? Plant some apple seeds from a freshly picked apple and some apple seeds that were in cold storage for several months. Try the same thing with peach and grape seeds. See what happens!

Acorns

It may take a while for the acorns to sprout, but wouldn't it be fun to grow your own little oak tree and then transplant it to your yard? Why not give it a try!

Remember: Planting in a glass is a fun, short-term project. Why not consider transplanting young plants into flower pots, other containers, or outside into the garden for extended life. (See Transplanting Fun, page 98.)

IDEAS

Plants need soil, sun, and water. Try the following experiments. See what happens. Observe and record what you see.

▪ *Let's See What Sun Does*

Plant three identical glasses of the seeds of your choice. When all three have sprouted, place one glass in a dark closet, one away from sunlight, and one on a sunny window sill. Now observe and record what you see. (Be sure to keep all three glasses watered so the soil will be damp.)

Example: Three glasses of lima beans planted 4/12/93— Experiment began 4/22/93

	Window Sill	**Closet**	**Dim Place**
4/29	Healthy, 4 inches tall	Pale color, not growing	Reaching toward the light
5/10	Growing	Dead	Small leaves
5/20	8 inches tall		Looking pale

You can learn so much by observing and recording! Perhaps you will want to do your recording in your Science Record Book. (See page 4.)

▪ *Let's See What Water Does*

Plant two identical glasses of seeds. Leave them both on the window sill. Keep both glasses damp until the seeds sprout. After they have sprouted, water one glass and don't water the other glass. Observe and record what you see.

Continued.

■ *Let's See What Soil Does*

Transplant a healthy lima bean plant. See Transplanting Fun below.

Compare the growth of your lima bean plant that is growing in soil with the limas growing in the jar in Watch Seeds Grow Before Your Eyes on page 101. Observe and record what you see.

Use your imagination! Try experiments **you** think of. Keep more charts and records.

Transplanting Fun

It is great fun to transplant the small plants that have sprouted in your plastic cups (see page 93) into bigger containers so they can live longer. Sometimes flowers and even fruits or vegetables will grow on these transplanted plants. We have had bean plants produce new beans and beautiful morning glories bloom in our classroom. (In spring and summer you can transplant directly to your yard.)

You Need:

4-inch or larger clay pots or milk, cottage cheese, or yogurt containers (either plastic or wax covered). They are waterproof, so they make great planters.

How To:

Cut any size milk carton or jug in half and use plastic and wax containers as they are. Put drainage rocks or small pieces of a broken clay flower pot in the bottom of the clay pots. Add potting soil and vermiculite or sand mixture (see page 93) and transplant your small plants into these larger containers. Seeds may be planted directly into them too.

Remember: Don't overwater. Just keep the soil damp.

Do you want to get fancy? Before planting you may want to decorate the outside of your containers with wrapping paper, fabric scraps, gay bandannas, or anything decorative for a very attractive look. You could even use a half gallon wax milk carton, cut window flaps, line with clear plastic wrap fastened with tape, and then maybe you would see the roots!

Make saucers of larger containers or use small trays to protect the window sill from spills.

Find That Baby Plant!

How To:

1. Use some of the large dried lima beans which you purchased to plant.

2. Let everyone feel these dried beans and notice the hard covering and the size differences.

3. Soak some of these beans overnight. Soak enough beans so everyone will have five or more. They swell up, so cover with lots of cool water.

4. The next day drain the water off, sit around a table, and examine the soaked beans.

5. Pass around at least one dried bean and several soaked beans to everyone.

6. Talk about how much bigger the soaked beans are and notice that the hard covers (skins) are now soft.

7. Now everyone can gently scratch and loosen the skins with your fingernails and gently peel off the skins.

8. The beans will open in two pieces if you gently pry them apart.

9. Now look for the baby plant, called the **embryo,** hiding inside. Some embryos fall out in the bag, so continue to open beans until everyone finds an embryo.

 10. The children will enjoy learning the word embryo. These beans can be used in your bean soup! (See page 188.)

Continued.

More Sunny Window Sill Fun

▪ *Letter Growing*

Sow seeds in the shape of letters of the alphabet. It is fun to plant the initials of the gardener.

How To:

Use wild bird seed mix (except the sunflower seeds) or radish seeds. Scratch the letters in the soil with a stick. Sow seeds thickly within these scratch marks. (Try using tweezers or a small spoon for this job.) Cover lightly with more soil. Keep the soil damp but not soggy. After the seeds sprout, remove the ones that have grown in the wrong places.

Helpful Hint: This idea would be too difficult for young children because it is tricky to plant only in the scratch marks. Young children will enjoy planting birdseed and radish seeds and might enjoy using tweezer's to pick up the seeds and drop them into the soil at random or in any pattern they wish to make.

▪ *Grow a Lentil Forest*

This is a great idea and you get to eat it too.

How To:

Place a handful of lentils in a shallow dish. Put in just enough water to cover the bottom of the dish. The lentils must ***not*** float in the water. Set the dish on a sunny window sill. Add enough water each day to keep the lentils damp. A mist spray bottle works well. Have fun watching your lentil forest grow! You can eat these sprouts and soft seeds in a salad if you wish.

▪ *Sweet Potato Fun*

A sweet potato will grow into a delightful trailing vine that you can train to go around your window frame. It may last as long as 18 months. A sweet potato vine lives so long because the plant uses the sweet potato as its food. The corn and lima seeds used in Watch Seeds Grow Before Your Eyes on page 101 will not grow too long (unless transplanted into soil) because their food source inside the lima and corn seeds is small. Growing a sweet potato used to be a never-fail project. However, in today's world, sweet potatoes are sometimes sprayed with sprout inhibitor, so follow the How To directions carefully for the best chance at success.

How To:

1. Select a plump sweet potato (or perhaps select and start two or three).

2. If possible, select one that already shows tiny purple buds at the top end. The top end sometimes has a grouping of small "eyes" that go around the potato.

3. Wash the potato with warm water and a sponge, dry it well, and place it in a completely dark place for three days.

4. Poke three strong toothpicks into the sweet potato halfway between the top and bottom and place it in a glass jar so that the bottom half will be submerged in water. The toothpicks support the potato on the rim of the jar.

5. Set your plant-to-be in a light but not too sunny window until it starts to grow. Be sure to keep the jar filled up and change the water now and then.

6. Keep your potato near a sunny window so the leaves will get some sun. Enjoy your beautiful trailing sweet potato vine. This can also be used as a hanging plant near a sunny window.

▪ Watch Seeds Grow Before Your Eyes— Observe and Enjoy

1. Wet a piece of white blotter or folded white heavy paper towel.

2. Press this around the interior of a clear glass jar. (A glass jar about 4 1/2 inches tall and 3 1/2 inches wide is perfect, but any jar will do.) Packaged garden limas will probably

Continued.

grow better than those sold in the grocery store's dried bean section.

3. Carefully push several large dried lima beans and Indian corn seeds between the paper and the glass. Be sure that several of the seeds are upside down so you can observe what happens.

4. Put sand in the jar to hold the paper and the seeds in place. Keep the sand damp.

5. Put the jar lid on and set the jar on the window sill with the beans and corn seeds facing the light of the sun.

6. Watch for growth and maybe mold.

7. If you see mold, look up the word *mold* and learn about it.

8. After growth begins, remove the lid and leave it off.

9. Keep the sand and paper moist and see how tall the plants will grow. Once the food in the seed is used up, the plant cannot grow very well. Compare the growth of these seeds with some seeds that are growing in soil. Make notes in your Science Record Book.

▪ Root Top Garden

1. Cut off the tops (about 3/4 inch) of some root vegetables. (I know carrots and turnips are pretty. Try others, too.)

2. Place them in a shallow dish with water 1/4 inch deep.

3. Add water daily so the dish is never dry.

4. Enjoy the pretty leaves that will appear.

▪ Carrot on a Cardboard

1. Look for a nice plump carrot.

2. Secure it with masking tape onto a sturdy piece of cardboard.

3. Place it on the cardboard so there will be room to write the children's comments about the changes.

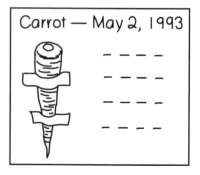

Carrot — May 2, 1993

4. Draw around the carrot so everyone will remember the carrot's original size.

5. Prop the carrot up against the wall and watch for changes.

6. Talk about the changes in size, color, smell, and feel and try to decide why this carrot changed so much.

■ *Make a Family or Class Seed Chart*

Watch for and glue many different kinds of seeds onto any size

piece of sturdy cardboard. You or the child will print the kind of seed and the person's name (who found the seed) next to the seed. Tape on large seeds (like peach) and put a ? next to unknown seeds.

■ *Discover Seeds and Other Plant Parts That We Eat*

The children may not realize that people eat—

SEEDS: beans, peas, corn

ROOTS: carrots, radishes, beets

STEMS: celery, asparagus

LEAVES: lettuce, cabbage, spinach

FRUITS: apples, oranges, pears

Visit the produce department! Buy—

1. Pea pods and string beans for the children to open and taste.

2. Popcorn (on the cob) for everyone to shell, pop, and eat.

3. Strawberries (with seeds on the outside) and other fruits. Let everyone chop up fruits (use table knives) for fruit salad.

4. Root vegetables that grow under the ground— carrots, beets, turnips. Enjoy a Tasting Party, perhaps with a favorite dip, and save those tops. (See Root Top Garden, page 102.)

Continued.

▪ *Fun with Sprouts! Nutritious and Delicious*

You Need:

1. A pint-size "zipper" plastic bag
2. A twistie tie
3. A fat, large needle
4. 2 tablespoons alfalfa seeds—buy at a health food store.

How To:

1. Punch at least 10 drain holes in the bottom seam and low sides of the bag with the needle.
2. Punch a hole near the top of the bag and insert the twistie tie. (Slip this over your sink faucet when draining the seeds.)
3. Ask a child to measure 2 level tablespoons alfalfa seeds and put them in the bag.
4. Zip up the bag and place it in a bowl of water to soak overnight.
5. The next day, drain the seeds and put them in a light place—but not in direct sunlight.
6. For the next 3 or 4 days, open the bag and add water to rinse the seeds. Drain again and place the bag in indirect light.
7. The last day, place the bag in direct sunlight to green up the sprouts.
8. Store in the same bag in the refrigerator.
9. Eat and enjoy.

SUGGESTED READINGS

Gage, Wilson. *Mrs. Gaddy and the Fast-Growing Vine*. New York: Greenwillow Books, 1985.

Gibbons, Gail. *Farming*. New York: Holiday House, 1988.

King, Elizabeth. *The Pumpkin Patch*. New York: Dutton Children's Books, 1990.

Krauss, Ruth. *The Carrot Seed*. New York: Harper & Row, 1945.

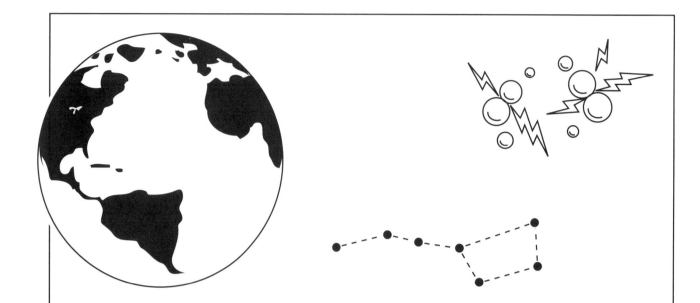

Chapter 7
The Wonders of Our World

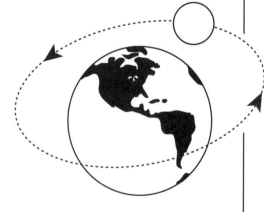

Our world is such a wonder with its water and its sky.
Miracles are everywhere and make us question "why?"

Children are full of questions about the world around them.

Why is the sky blue? Why does it snow? Why can't we see a rainbow everyday? Why? Why? Why?

Let's have some fun trying to understand: What is the Earth like? What about our sky? Why is water so wonderful?

THE SOLAR SYSTEM

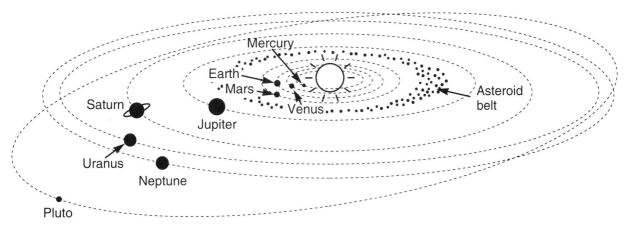

Our planet **Earth** is one of nine planets that travel around our sun. The nine planets and other heavenly bodies that revolve around our sun make up our **solar system.** Since **solar** means sun, you could call it the "sun system"! (See Make Playdough Planets, page 112.)

Stars

FACTS

- Our **sun** is really a huge star. **Stars** are made of hot gases that burn and give off heat and light. Planets do not make their own heat or give off light.

- OUR SUN IS SO BRIGHT WE MUST NEVER LOOK AT IT DIRECTLY BECAUSE IT WOULD HURT OUR EYES.

- The planet Earth gets all its light, heat, and energy from our sun.

- Our sun is so big that more than 1 million Earths could fit inside of it. (See Idea, How Big Is Our Sun? page 109.)

- Some stars are even bigger and brighter than our sun.

- Other stars look small because they are so far away from planet Earth. If we could see them up close, we would see that stars are many different sizes and colors (red, yellow, white, and blue), and some stars are brighter than others.

- Stars seem to twinkle because their light is shining down through layers of moving air.

- Stars shine all the time, but we see them only at night because in the daytime our sun outshines the light of the other stars.

- A **shooting star** is really not a star at all! It is a lump of rock or metal, usually from the asteroid belt (see the picture on page 107). It falls so fast into our air that it begins to burn and looks like a streak of light.

- Scientists call shooting stars **meteors;** if they hit the ground, they are called **meteorites.**

- Most meteorites are baseball size or smaller, but a few have been bigger than a 10-story building. When a giant meteorite hits the ground, it breaks into tiny pieces and makes a huge hole (crater) in the ground.

IDEAS

Become a Star Watcher

Lie down on a blanket and watch the stars. See how they seem to move even in the time from early evening to later that same night. The stars are moving but their movement is not noticeable to our eyes. It is the Earth's movement that causes a star's position to look different to us in such a short period of time.

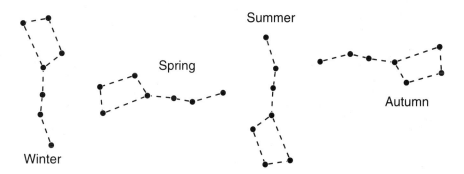

Spring

Summer

Autumn

Winter

Notice that the Big Dipper can always be seen, but its position in the sky seems to change.

Borrow or buy a basic book on star watching such as the *Golden Nature Guide* called *Stars.*

How Big Is Our Sun?

You Need:

1. A round bowl or a whiffle ball or any old ball you can cut a hole in.
2. A bag of small, dried beans (like navy beans).

How To:

1. First remember our sun is so big that more than 1 million planets the size of Earth could fit inside of it.
2. Pretend that your round object is the size of our sun and that each one of the dried beans is the size of our planet Earth.
3. Count as you drop one bean ("Earth") at a time into your make-believe sun. You won't get to 1 million, but this activity will help everyone understand that our sun is much larger than our Earth, and it is great counting practice too! ☺

Gravity

Our sun has a special force called **gravity,** which keeps the planets moving around it and stops them from floating away into space. The Earth has gravity too. **Earth's gravity** is the force that pulls all objects toward the center of the Earth. The other planets have gravity too—larger planets usually have more, and smaller planets have less gravity.

IDEA

Have Fun with Gravity

- Children enjoy jumping as high as they can, dropping pebbles, balls, and leaves from the top of a climber, rolling a toy car down a wooden ramp, sliding down a slide, swinging on a swing. Gravity makes us stop swinging (unless we pump), since its force pulls us and all objects back down to the ground.
- See how long you and the children can hold your arms straight out at shoulder height. Explain it is the pull of gravity that makes you tired.
- See if the children know why they cannot jump higher. (Gravity pulls us back down.)
- Help children understand that without the force of gravity, our world would be a very different place.

Planets

FACTS
- All the planets move in somewhat circular (elliptical) paths (called **orbits**) around our sun.
- Earth is the only planet known to have life.

- **Mercury** is the planet nearest to the sun, with Venus, Earth, Mars, Jupiter, Saturn, Uranus, Neptune, and Pluto following in that order.

    Sue Einig's 4th grade class at St. Joseph's School in Manchester, Missouri, uses this wonderful sentence to help us remember this order:

    My **V**ery **E**nergetic **M**other **J**ust **S**erved **U**s **N**ine **P**izzas.

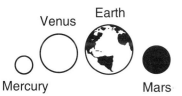

Venus Earth
Mercury Mars
The four inner planets

- The **four inner planets** (Mercury, Venus, Earth, and Mars) are all hard and rocky.

- **Asteroids** (chunks of rocks and metal that are in orbit around the sun) are in between the inner four and outer five planets. Scientists call the space between the fourth and fifth planets the **asteroid belt.** (See Facts, page 108, about Shooting Stars.)

- **Mars** looks red up in the sky because of the rusty iron in its soil.

- **Jupiter** is the largest planet. In our solar system only our sun is larger than Jupiter.

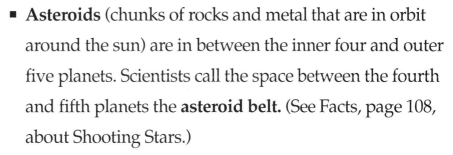

Jupiter

- **Saturn** is the second largest planet. It is very cold and has three **rings** around it that may be ice crystals. Some other planets also have rings.

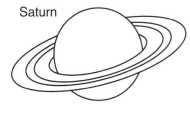

Saturn

- **Pluto** is the smallest planet.

For more fun facts, borrow from the library or buy *The Magic School Bus Lost in the Solar System* by Joanna Cole (New York: Scholastic Inc.). It is an entertaining way to find out all about our solar system.

IDEA

Make Playdough Planets

Even young children will enjoy making their own solar system on stiff cardboard.

You Need:

1. A sturdy cardboard circle (Frozen pizza is often packaged on a cardboard circle.)
2. Playdough (see page 191 for the recipe) to make balls that will be the sun and the nine planets.
3. Blue crayon or marker (if you wish to color the "sky" blue)
4. Tempera paint (optional) to paint the sun and planets
5. Small pebbles (for asteroids)
6. Glue

How To:

1. If you decide to color the cardboard blue, that should be done first.
2. Explain to the children that they will need to make one golf-ball-size playdough ball to be the sun and nine smaller balls of various sizes to be the nine planets. Some children will want to try to make their balls to match the facts; some will just have fun gluing on their sun and balls without concern about size. This should be each child's choice. If you decide to paint the balls, let the paint dry completely before gluing them on. If pebbles are used for the asteroids, they can be painted or left plain.
3. Glue the sun and planets onto the cardboard using a generous blob of glue (Elmer's type will work fine) for each.
4. Remind the children who are adding the asteroid belt to place the pebbles around the sun after the fourth planet away from the sun (Mars).
5. Allow adequate drying time.

Children enjoy showing their very own solar system and sharing their new knowledge with adults!

THE MOON

- Some planets in our solar system have many moons (Saturn has at least 17), but Earth has only one.

- The moon has no air, no water, no signs of life.

- The moon's surface is rock and sand with many large **craters** (bowl-shaped holes) formed millions of years ago when the moon was hit by meteorites. (See page 108.)

- The moon has much less gravity than the Earth. People feel very light, can jump very high, and can lift and carry very heavy objects while they are on the moon.

- The moon is very hot in the daytime and very cold at night.

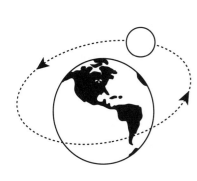

- The moon travels around the Earth, just as the Earth travels around the sun.

- It takes one month for the moon to go around the earth one time.

- The moon does not make any light of its own, so the moonlight we see is really light from the sun that hits the moon and then bounces off, the way light is reflected from a mirror.

- The moon seems to change shape. When the moon moves between the Earth and the sun we see no moon at all. This is known as the new moon. As the moon travels around the Earth, the whole round moon is always up in the sky, but sometimes we see only part of it. The rest of the moon is hidden by the shadow of the Earth. Everyone loves a full moon!

I recommend you borrow or buy the book *The Moon Seems to Change* by Franklyn M. Branley (Crowell, 1987). Its appealing illustrations and simple text make understanding the phases of the moon easy and enjoyable.

IDEAS

Walk in the Moonlight

Take a walk in a very dark place during the time of the full moon. You will be surprised how much light comes from the moon. You won't need a flashlight!

Become a Moonwatcher

It is fun to watch the moon and notice all its changing shapes.

New   Crescent   First Quarter   Full   Third Quarter   Crescent   New

Take a Make-Believe Trip to the Moon

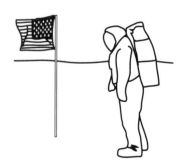

Children love to hear about astronauts and their trips to the moon! On July 20, 1969, human beings first set foot on the moon during the flight of Apollo 11. This was the first of six United States lunar landings. The last landing was in 1972.

You Need:

The ability to pretend and have fun as you act-out taking a trip to the moon.

How To:

1. Talk to the children about what the moon is like. (See Facts, page 113.)

2. Put on your spacesuits, strap yourselves into the spaceship (there is no gravity in space, so you will float around if not strapped in.)

3. Get ready for the blast off. Everyone counts down 10, 9, 8, 7, 6, 5, 4, 3, 2, 1, zero, blast off!

4. Enjoy the beautiful view of planet Earth from the spaceship; take pictures; squeeze food and drinks into your mouth; turn the dials on your control panels; take a spacewalk. (Remember to attach a strong cord onto your belt so you won't float way in space.)

5. Arrive at the moon, check your air tanks, place a pole with the American flag into the rocky soil, bounce up and down and pretend to be very light, pick up heavy rocks, collect a few rocks to take home.

6. Take a good look around to see if you can find any water or signs of life; take lots of pictures, and get ready to get back into the spaceship for the ride home.

7. Check with mission control to see if everything is all set for your landing. Three giant parachutes will open up and let you drift gently down into the ocean. A helicopter will pick you up and carry you to a nearby ship. Safe at home! What a thrilling, wonderful adventure!

DAY AND NIGHT

The spinning of the Earth makes night and day. Our Earth is the shape of a ball and is always turning as it moves around the sun. When your part of the Earth is turned away from the sun, you have night. When it is turned toward the sun, you have day.

It takes 24 hours for the Earth to make one complete spin.

IDEA

See Night and Day Before Your Eyes

You Need:

1. A flashlight (your make-believe sun)
2. An apple (poke a pencil through the apple to act as a handle for you to hold as you turn it)
3. A map pin and a thumb tack (or two different colors of thumbtacks or map pins)

How To:

1. Tell the children our Earth always spins from west to east (counterclockwise).
2. Pretend the apple is our Earth and the flashlight is the sun.
3. Stick the map pin into your make-believe Earth at the place where you live.
4. Stick the thumbtack in the "Earth" on the other side of the Earth from where you live.
5. Darken the room and turn on the make-believe sun. The "sun" will not move, so have someone hold the flashlight in one place.
6. Begin to slowly turn the "Earth" counterclockwise so that everyone can see why we have night and day. Notice early morning and evening as the sun seems to rise and set. Remember: the sun does not really rise and set. **The Earth is moving, not the sun!**
7. Notice that the people on the other side of the Earth are having day when we are having night and night when we are having day!

Remember: A day is 24 hours. That is how long it takes for our Earth to turn around one time.

SEASONS

- The planet Earth spins as it travels all the way around the sun.

- It takes one year (365 spins) for it to go around the sun one time.

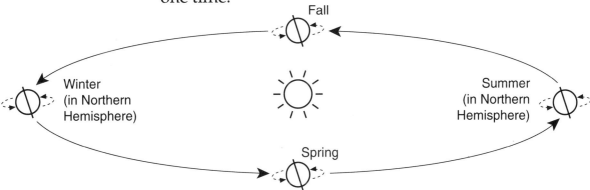

- As it spins, it moves from west to east (counterclockwise) and is tilted on its **axis** (an imaginary line drawn through the Earth from pole to pole).

- The "tilt" of the Earth always stays the same.

- The days are longer and we get more direct sunlight when our part of the Earth is tilted toward the sun. This is the season we call **summer.**

- We have shorter days and get less direct sunlight when the Earth is tilted away from the sun. This season is called **winter.**

- **Spring** and **fall** are the nice times between summer and winter.

IDEAS

See the Earth Travel Around the Sun

You Need:

1. A grapefruit to be the sun

2. A soda bottle or a vase to hold up the "sun"

3. An apple to be the Earth (with a pencil poked through to act as a handle)

How To:

Slowly spin the apple Earth counterclockwise as you move it all the way around the grapefruit sun.

See the Moon Travel Around the Earth

After you play this game maybe you will always remember that our moon travels around the Earth and the Earth travels around the sun.

You Need:

1. A golf ball to be the moon (stick a map pin in the ball to act as a handle as you turn it)

2. A grapefruit sun

3. An apple Earth

4. Strips of colored crepe paper to be "stars" (optional)

How To:

1. Have one person hold the grapefruit sun. This person stands still.

2. Have the person holding the apple Earth walk around the "sun," turning slowly counterclockwise as he or she goes.

3. Have someone hold the golf ball moon and walk around the "Earth," turning slowly counterclockwise as he or she goes.

If more children are present, they can sit in a circle and shake the strips of crepe paper, pretending to be twinkling stars.

You could add eight more people to move around the sun pretending to be the other planets, and then you would have our whole solar system. (Don't forget the asteroid belt!) Try not to get dizzy!

AIR

The planet Earth is wrapped in a layer of air, which is called the **atmosphere.** There are many different gases in our air. One of them is **oxygen,** which is the gas people and other animals need to live. Another gas is **carbon dioxide,** which plants need to live. (See page 25.)

- You cannot see or taste or smell fresh air, but *we can't live without it!*

- The air in our sky looks colored because sunlight is really a mixture of colors (see Rainbows, page 135.) A *clear sky looks blue* because the blue rays are the only rays of light that come through for our eyes to see. At *sunrise and sunset the sky often looks red* because the red rays show the most. At these times of day, clouds and dust in the air may also be beautiful colors. Astronauts tell us the sky is black in outer space, which is above the earth's air (atmosphere).

- Air is always moving. Warm air is lighter than cold air, so it rises. Air pressure changes cause our **winds.** A gentle wind is called a **breeze;** a very strong wind is called a **hurricane.**

- Air has weight, but we cannot feel it unless the wind is blowing it against us.

- Air is kept in place by the Earth's gravity. (See Gravity, page 110.)

- Air (the atmospheric layer known as **ozone**) protects us from the sun's dangerous ultraviolet rays and acts like a huge blanket, keeping warm air near the Earth both night and day.

Have Fun Learning About Air

- **Air is Real**

You Need:

1. A clear container about 2/3 full with water

2. A paper napkin or paper towel

3. A small juice glass

How To:

Put a paper napkin or tissue into a clear juice glass. Turn the glass over and quickly push it straight down into the container of water. Pull the glass out quickly, straight up. The tissue or napkin will be dry because air has kept the water from getting into the glass. Put the glass straight down again. This time tilt the glass to one side; notice bubbles of air escaping. Now that the air is gone, there is room for the water to enter the glass and to wet the tissue or towel!

- **Air Holds Water**

You Need:

1. Water

2. People's fingers

3. Small blackboard

How To:

Ask everyone to dip one finger in a bowl of water. Ask, "How can we dry our fingers without wiping them off?" Blowing or swinging them in the air will help the water go into the air. Also watch water disappear as a blackboard dries. Tell the children water on their fingers and on the blackboard has **evaporated.** (See page 129 for explanation of evaporation.)

- **Air Takes up Space**

You Need:

A balloon, a small plastic baggie, or a small paper bag

How To:

Blow air into a balloon, a small plastic baggie, or a small paper bag. The children will be able to *"see"* and *"feel"* the enclosed air and know that air takes up space. They can feel the air as it comes out of the balloon.

- ### Fire Needs the Oxygen in Air to Burn

You Need:

1. 2 birthday candles
2. 2 candle holders and 2 balls of playdough
3. 2 index cards
4. A clear glass jar
5. A toilet paper or paper towel roll

BE SURE CHILDREN UNDERSTAND THAT ONLY ADULTS OR OLDER CHILDREN MAY DO THIS IDEA.

How To:

1. Stick two balls of playdough onto two index cards. (See playdough, page 191.)
2. Place the two birthday candles in the two plastic candle holders and the candle holders into the playdough balls. The playdough balls will hold up the candle holders.
3. Light the candles (AN ADULT JOB).
4. Place a clear glass jar over one burning candle and a cardboard paper towel roll over the other burning candle.
5. Watch what happens. When the candle has used all the oxygen in the air in the jar, the candle will go out.
6. After the candle covered by the jar has gone out, carefully lift the paper towel roll up to find that candle still burning. Why?
7. Tell the children the carbon dioxide in a person's breath will put out the other candle. The children will help blow it out!

Continued.

▪ Blow Painting is Fun

You Need:

1. Medicine droppers (see note, page 132)
2. Different colors of tempera paint
3. Straws
4. Paper

How To:

Children or adults use medicine droppers to drop different colors of tempera paint onto paper. The children blow through straws to move the drops of paint into designs. Their carbon dioxide (the air people breath out) has helped make an interesting picture.

▪ Air is a Force

Find out how air helps us drink through a straw.

You Need:

1. A drinking glass half full of water
2. A straw for each person

How To:

1. Put your straw in the water.
2. Suck up the air out of your straw. As you do this, more air pushes down on the water in the glass and helps push the water up the straw! Air is a force.

Explain that the force of air also makes sail boats move across the water, horns blow, bicycle pumps and vacuum cleaners work, windmills turn, airplanes fly, and much more.

▪ Blow Bubbles

Bubbles are bits of air trapped inside a liquid ball. Have fun blowing bubbles!

You Need:

1. A glass of water and a straw for each person
2. A few drops of dishwashing liquid in each glass for added fun

3. A shallow tray or pie pan

4. A tin can with both ends removed. (BE SURE THERE ARE NO SHARP PLACES ON THE CAN.)

How To:

1. Blow air into your straw, causing your water to form bubbles.

2. Add soap and get more bubbles.

3. Put your soapy water into a shallow tray or pie pan. Make really big bubbles by blowing long and gently into your straw when the straw is only partly under the water.

4. Touch your big bubble with a wet finger. Then touch it with a dry finger. Do you agree that bubbles are more fragile (break more easily) when they touch something dry?

5. Look for colors in your bubbles.

6. Try dipping your tin can into the soapy water so that you get a soap film at one end. Blow gently on the other end to form a bubble. Aren't bubbles fun?

WATER—WE CAN'T LIVE WITHOUT IT

Our Earth is the only planet in our solar system that has water. Look at a world globe and you can see that water covers nearly 70% of the Earth's surface. Only 3% is freshwater, and most of this freshwater is locked up in solar ice caps and glaciers. *We must take good care of the small amount of freshwater we have to use.*

The Water Cycle

Did you know that we are using the very same water the dinosaurs used? The Earth's water is used over and over in the water cycle:

1. The sun heats the water in the lakes, rivers, and seas.

2. The heated water turns into moisture (water vapor) in the air. This is called **evaporation.**

3. As the moisture rises it cools and joins together to make clouds.

4. Sometimes there is so much moisture in the clouds that it turns back into water and falls out of the clouds as rain or sometimes as different forms of ice. This never ending circle is called **the water cycle.**
   (Remember to pretend to be rain, see page 126.)

Clouds

A **cloud** is a great cluster of tiny water droplets or ice crystals that you can see in the sky. It takes billions of ice crystals to make up a cloud. (See The Water Cycle, above).

TYPES OF CLOUDS

Become a cloud watcher and you will see that there are many different kinds of clouds. The following are the most common types of clouds:

Cirrus

  Cirrus: thin, wispy white curls formed by ice crystals found *high* above other clouds.

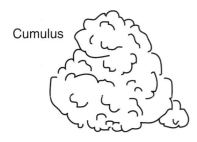

Cumulus

Cumulus: white and puffy like heaps of cotton, most often occurring in spring or summer.

Stratus: thin, grayish white layers of clouds found *low* in the sky.

Stratus

Nimbostratus: long, flat, dark gray clouds that often bring rain.

Nimbostratus

It is fun to check the sky each day and watch the ever changing scene. (See Watch the Sky, page 13.) Clouds sometimes bring us wet weather.

Rain

Raindrops form in clouds when tiny water droplets join together or when larger ice crystals melt.

A raindrop must contain about 1,000 droplets to be heavy enough to fall to Earth.

Ice from the Sky

Snow. It snows when the crystals of frozen water come out of the cloud at about 32 degrees Fahrenheit, the freezing point of water. Each snowflake has its own special design, but all snowflakes have six points.

Sleet. When rain falls through a layer of super-cold air and is frozen before reaching the ground, it falls as sleet.

Freezing Rain. Rain that freezes as it touches something cold is called freezing rain.

Hail. A hailstone really starts as a piece of dust or dirt. Ice crystals grow on this as it is tossed up and down in the cloud—as many as 25 times! Water freezes on the crystals in layers. If you could cut a hailstone in half, it would look like this.

 Some hailstones get as big as golf balls, baseballs, and grapefruit! Look out if they hit your car or your head!

IDEAS

Pretend to Be Rain

Children enjoy pretending to be drops of water in a puddle, evaporating up into the sky, cooling off, and coming together with other water drops in a cloud, then falling back down to Earth as rain, snow, sleet, or hail. Maybe your "rain" will fall in the garden.

Make Your Own Rain

THIS IDEA IS AN ADULT JOB.

You Need:

1. A tea kettle
2. A hot plate or heat from any cooking stove
3. A saucepan and ice cubes

How To:

1. Explain to the children that water droplets in the air come together and grow in size when the air becomes colder. When they get too heavy to float in the air, they fall as rain.
2. Heat the water in the tea kettle until steam is coming out of the spout. KEEP THE CHILDREN AWAY FROM THE STEAM.
3. Show the children the pan bottom is dry; then put in the ice cubes.
4. Hold the saucepan filled with ice cubes in the steam and watch the "rain" form and fall.

Look Carefully at Snowflakes

You Need:

1. Snow falling from the sky
2. A piece of black construction paper (or a black sock will do)
3. A freezer
4. A magnifying glass (optional)

How To:

1. When the snowflakes begin to fall, put your black paper in the freezer for a few minutes so it can get very cold.
2. Quickly remove it from the freezer, dash outside, and let some snowflakes fall on your paper.
3. Look at their beautiful shapes with your eyes or a magnifying glass.

Do you see their six points? Can you find two that are just alike? Scientists tell us that every snowflake is different but that they all have six points!

Let's Have Fun with Water

- Talk to the children about where your drinking water comes from. (Find out if you don't know by calling your water company.) Inquire if a tour of your water works is possible. Read *The Magic School Bus at the Waterworks* by Joanna Cole.
- Visit ponds, lakes, rivers, and oceans whenever possible.
- Act out Seeing Is Believing on page 147.

Discover that Water Can Be in 3 Forms:
Liquid, Gas, and Solid

- **Liquid**

Children learn about pouring at a very early age. They see grownups pouring their milk and juice. At bath time children love to pour water from one cup to another. At school, water play is always a favorite activity.

Let's introduce the word *liquid* to children.

Continued.

You Need:

1. 2 plastic glasses

2. A small pitcher of water

How To:

1. Tell the children to watch while you have some fun with water.

2. Pour some water from the pitcher, filling one glass about half full.

3. Pour the water back and forth from one glass to another.

4. Ask the child or children, "What am I doing?" They will probably tell you, "Pouring the water."

5. Explain that anything you can pour has a special name. It is called a **liquid.** They will enjoy saying liquid.

6. Talk about other liquids that they see every day, such as milk, juice, coffee, and soda.

▪ Gas

Because they cannot see it, children do not usually know that there is water in the air. One way that you can help children see that this is true is by demonstrating ***how heated water turns into steam*** (a term many children know):

THIS IS AN ADULT JOB. BE SURE NO CHILD IS NEAR THE HEAT.

You Need:

1. Water

2. A small pan

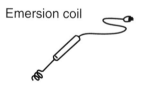
Emersion coil

3. A hot plate, a cooking stove, or an electric heat emersion coil (available at most hardware stores) works well. (If you use an emersion coil, the water can be put in a heavy glass jar.) Using clear glass allows everyone to see the bubble action and finally the boiling of the water.

How To:

1. Pour a small amount of water into your pan or jar.

2. Turn on the heat. Explain that when water is heated, the heat changes the liquid water to a gas. This is called **evaporation**—a nice "science word" for children to learn. When the water boils we see the gas. We call it steam. **Steam** is really liquid water that has turned into a gas. Tell the children that the "science word" for this gas is **water vapor.**

3. If you let the pan boil dry and then immediately turn it over to show the children that all the water you put in the pan is now up in the air, it helps them really see and understand that water can and does change into water vapor.

Also see the idea Air Holds Water, page 120.

▪ Solid

Pick up any object and explain that anything you can hold in your hand is called a solid. Ask the children if water can ever be a solid. Some children will say, "Yes, when it is ice." Other children will not have made that connection yet. In either case, it is fun to try this idea.

You Need:

A few ice cubes in a small covered thermos or a covered plastic container—something that will hide the ice cubes from view and let the ice cubes be heard when you shake the container.

How To:

1. Shake the container and wonder together what could be making that noise.
2. Listen to the children's guesses.
3. Open the container and hold up an ice cube.
4. Put it in your hand and say, "This frozen water must be a solid because I am holding it!"
5. Enjoy watching together as the solid water melts and turns back into a liquid.

 This simple activity must seem like magic to children because they always enjoy it.

Continued.

Evaporation (See explanation on page 129.)

You Need:

1. 2 small dishes that are alike (plastic jar lids will work)
2. Foil to make a cover for one dish
3. A teaspoon
4. A small amount of water colored with food coloring

How To:

Put several teaspoons of colored water into each dish. Cover one dish with foil; leave one uncovered. After an hour or so check to see what has happened. Has the uncovered water evaporated? See how long it takes for the covered water to evaporate.

If you set a third dish in direct sunlight or near a heat source, the children will see that ***heat speeds evaporation.***

Condensation

You Need:

1. A dry glass jar without a top
2. Ice cubes
3. A piece of colored paper

How To:

In front of the children put the ice cubes into the dry jar, set it aside, and check later to see what has happened. Water in the air near the cold jar cooled off, and water droplets formed on the outside of the glass.

Try setting the jar on a piece of colored paper. Does the paper get wet?

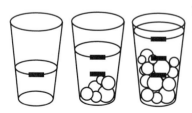

Water Displacement

You Need:

1. A large glass or plastic jar or bowl you can see through
2. Several sizes of rocks or heavy objects
3. A marking pen

How To:

1. Fill the container half full of water.

2. Mark the water line with your marker.

3. Put in the heaviest object and mark the higher water line.

4. Add more objects, making a mark after each addition.

5. Remove all the objects and see what happens.

It is fun to explain to the children that when they get into the bathtub, the water goes up because they displace the water!

Water Dissolves Sugar

You Need:

1. A small, clear juice glass

2. A spoonful of sugar

3. A spoon

4. Water

How To:

1. Each child fills a small glass half full of water, scoops up a spoonful of sugar, puts the sugar in the water, and stirs until the sugar is no longer showing. Tell the children the sugar has disappeared because it has **dissolved.** This is another great "science word."

2. The child can taste the water and know that the sugar is in there because it tastes sweet. You now have a **solution.**

3. If you want to see that spoonful of sugar again, boil the water until it has all evaporated or set the glass of sugar water in a sunny window and let the sun's heat do the evaporating!

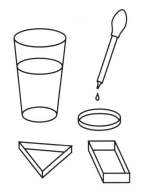

Does Water Have a Shape?

You Need:

1. Medicine droppers, one for each child (these are available at the drug store). Be sure to see note on page 132.

2. Square, round, rectangular, and triangle-shaped containers (jar and bottle caps work)

Continued.

3. A 6 oz plastic cup about 2/3 full of water for each child

4. Short straws

5. Old towels for wiping up

How To:

1. Put the different shapes of containers on a long low table.

2. Give each child his or her water and a medicine dropper.*

3. Ask the children to work together to fill up the containers with droppers full of water.

4. Ask what shape is water? Discover liquid takes the shape of the container it is in!

5. Give out straws and blow bubbles!

Water Has "Skin" (Surface Tension)

You Need:

1. Medicine droppers

2. Water

3. Waxed paper

4. Dishwashing detergent for the adult to use

How To:

While the children are having fun with the medicine droppers and straws (see above), put pieces of waxed paper down on the table so the children can drop water on the waxed paper. (Be sure you place the waxed paper where the table is dry.) Each water drop forms a ball. The outside of each drop is like a "skin." The children may decide to make designs with these drops.

*NOTE: Learning to use a medicine dropper is tricky for young children. **Don't** let this be a frustrating experience. Demonstrate how you must—

1. Squeeze the rubber bulb while the glass tip of the dropper is under the water.
2. Release your squeeze **before** taking the dropper out of the water.
3. Move the dropper over the container you are filling.
4. Again squeeze the bulb so the water can flow out.

After you demonstrate several times, it is fun for you to pretend you are a robot following the directions that the children give you to fill and release the dropper. This helps them learn the four steps. Stay with the child who is having a difficult time with this skill until he or she feels comfortable with it. After the children have used the droppers for awhile, give them each a straw. They will have fun blowing bubbles, and some children will discover fun ways to use the straws and droppers together.

Demonstrate how a drop of soap (dropped from a medicine dropper) will break the "skin" and the water will spread out. Fun!

Needle Float

This is tricky to do but fun when it works.

You Need:

1. A fork
2. A needle
3. A bowl of water

How To:

1. Lay the needle on the fork and let the needle roll gently into the water. It floats, making a dent in the water, again proving that water does have a "skin."
2. Now drop the needle point down into the bowl. The point breaks the "skin," and the needle drops to the bottom.

Freeze Water

You Need:

1. A plastic container
2. Water
3. A freezer

How To:

1. Carefully fill a plastic container to the top with water.
2. Place it in the freezer or outside (if it's below freezing outside).
3. Let the children see how the water rises above the top of the container when frozen. This shows everyone that water **expands** (gets bigger) when it freezes.
4. Let the container sit at room temperature to thaw so the children can see it return to its original water level.

Is Water Always Wet?

Find out why you don't get wet when you fall on the ice.

Continued.

You Need:

1. An ice cube

2. A piece of colored paper

How To:

1. Touch the ice to the paper and notice the paper is still dry.

2. Continue to gently rub the ice on the paper. You will notice that only when the ice begins to melt does the paper get wet. **Ice is dry water!**

Sink and Float

You Need:

Various items you find in the house such as—

1. A wooden block

2. A plastic lid

3. A 2- by 2-inch flat piece of foil

4. A film can

5. A clothespin

6. A twistie tie

7. A marble-size ball of playdough

8. A dishpan or other large tub of water

9. 2 plastic trays—one marked "sink" and the other "float"

How To:

Have fun trying each item to see if it sinks or floats.

There are two ways to play this game:

1. Begin with all your objects in one container. Then place each item on the appropriate tray after you try it.

2. Guess ahead of time as you put the items on the sink and float trays. Then play the sink or float game and see if you guessed right when you placed them on the trays.

It is tricky to guess what some items will do, but it is always fun to play the Sink and Float Game!

Lightning and Thunder

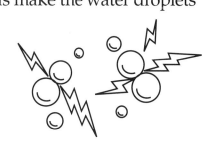

- During a storm, strong winds make the water droplets in clouds rub against each other. This causes sparks of electricity, called **lightning,** that shoot out of the cloud.

- Lightning is very hot. It heats the air around it. As the hot air pushes out against the cooler air, it makes a loud noise called **thunder.**

- *Thunder is just a lot of hot air* and cannot hurt you, but *lightning can be very dangerous.*

IDEA

Learn Lightning Safety Rules

- Never stand under a tree during a storm.
- Leave swimming pools, lakes, ball fields, and golf courses if you see lightning or if a storm is coming.
- Go into a building (not a shed or metal building) or a hard topped car (not a convertible).
- Keep windows and doors shut.
- Stay away from faucets, sinks, tubs, windows, doors, and television sets. (Pull the plug on the TV.)
- Don't talk on the phone or use electrical appliances.
- If you are in an open field, crouch down but do not lie down.

RAINBOWS

- Light is really a mixture of many beautiful colors.
- A rainbow forms only when the sun is shining and it is raining at the same time.

- When sunlight shines through rain drops, the raindrops bend the light so we can see all these beautiful colors in a rainbow up in the sky.

- There are seven colors in the rainbow, and they are always in the same order. From bottom to top—violet, indigo, blue, green, yellow, orange, and red.

- The colors blend together, so it is difficult to pick out seven colors.

- Every rainbow is really a complete circle! When we see a rainbow, it looks like an arch because the ground and trees get in the way of our seeing the whole circle.

- From an airplane or a high mountain the rainbow would look like this. (I have a friend who saw several circle rainbows from mountains in Hawaii!)

- Rainbows happen only when the sun is low in the sky and all conditions are just right.

- If you are very lucky and look very closely, you may get to see a **double rainbow.** A second rainbow sometimes forms above the bright rainbow. Its colors are always dull, and the order of its colors is reversed so that from bottom to top you will see—red, orange, yellow, green, blue, indigo, and violet. Isn't that amazing! (I have seen several double rainbows, so I know that this is true.)

IDEAS

Make Your Own Rainbows

▪ In a Dark Room

You Need:

1. A prism or a crystal chandelier drop
2. A flashlight
3. A dark room

How To:

Children love to sit on the floor in a dark room and see rainbows form on the walls and ceiling as you shine the light from the flashlight through the prism or crystal. Fun!

▪ Outside

You Need:

1. A sunny day
2. A garden hose

How To:

With your back to the sun, spray water from the hose into the air and watch for the rainbow!

▪ With Popsicle Sticks

You Need:

1. 7 popsicle sticks
2. Water colors or markers in the seven rainbow colors (indigo is a very deep shade of blue)
3. Cardboard
4. Glue

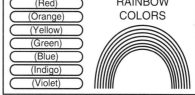

How To:

The children color their popsicle sticks, glue them on their piece of cardboard with the colors in the correct order (they will need help with this part), and decorate the cardboard any way they wish.

Continued.

■ **On Paper**

You Need:

1. Paint, crayons, markers, or chalk (try to include all the rainbow colors [indigo is a deep shade of blue])
2. Paper

How To:

Children love to make rainbow pictures! ***Don't*** insist they use the "correct" colors. Some children may want to follow nature's color order, and some will not. Some will use pink and many other shades. The main idea is to ***enjoy!***

Some children may decide to make a double rainbow.

Perhaps they will want to fold a sheet of paper and make a greeting card for someone they love.

Make a Collection of Rainbow Pictures

Watch for and collect rainbow pictures you will find in magazines, in advertisements, and on greeting cards. Add these rainbow pictures to those you and the children have made. Keep them in your Science Picture File (see page 18).

Sing These Simple Rainbow Songs

(Tune: *Twinkle, Twinkle, Little Star*)

Rainbow, rainbow way up high
Pretty in the summer sky.
Seven colors blend just right
Rainbow, rainbow what a sight!

Violet, indigo, blue, and green
Yellow, orange, and red are seen.
Rainbows come when things are just right
You'll never see a rainbow at night!

It is fun to clap as you sing this song and fun to let the children guess the last word, "night." To help everyone learn the song, let the children be your echo after you sing each line. Then you can sing the whole song all together. You can use your popsicle stick rainbows (see page 137) to help the children remember the color order.

Even very young children will enjoy this next rainbow song. The children echo the adult.

(Tune: *Frère Jacques [Brother John]*)

Adult	**Children**
See the rainbow	See the rainbow
In the sky	In the sky
Seven pretty colors	Seven pretty colors
Way up high	Way up high

Make a Rainbow Game

You Need:

1. A sheet of white paper 12 by 18 inches if available (a smaller sheet will also do)
2. Crayons or markers of the seven rainbow colors
3. Laminating machine (print shops and teacher supply stores provide laminating service).
4. Scissors

How To:

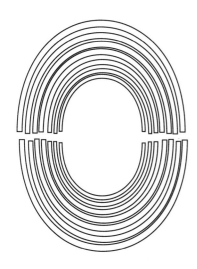

1. Make a rainbow with the colors in the correct order. (See Rainbows, page 136.)
2. Be sure each colored strip is about 1/2 to 3/4 inch wide.
3. Have this rainbow picture laminated.
4. Carefully cut apart the seven colors so you have seven arch-shaped pieces.
5. Pass out the different colors to seven children or family members. Some may have several colors.
6. Sitting on the floor, see if you can put the rainbow back together from bottom to top and then from top to bottom.
7. Sing the color part of the Rainbow Song to help you remember the correct color order.
8. Switch colors and play again. Fun!

Continued.

If you are doing this with a class of children, make as many laminated rainbows as you need so the class can divide into groups of seven and play the game all at the same time. Maybe two of the arch-shaped rainbows will fit together to make a circle rainbow!

SUGGESTED READINGS

Branley, Franklyn M. *The Moon Seems to Change.* New York: Thomas Y. Crowell, 1987.

Chisolm, Jane. *Finding Out About Our Earth.* London: Usborne Publishing Ltd., 1982.

Cole, Joanna. *The Magic School Bus at the Waterworks.* New York: Scholastic Inc., 1986.

Cole, Joanna. *The Magic School Bus Lost in the Solar System.* New York: Scholastic Inc., 1990.

Zim, Herbert S., and Baker, Robert H. *Stars.* A *Golden Nature Guide* Book. Racine, Wisconsin: Western Publishing Co., 1985.

Chapter 8
Give a Hoot About Litter, Pollution, and Recycling

Nobody makes a greater mistake than he who did nothing because he could only do a little.

EDMUND BURKE—BRITISH STATESMAN AND ORATOR

Our beautiful world is being littered, polluted, and spoiled. *If we all pitch in, we can make a difference.* So please, care, become aware, do your part.

Woodsy Owl is America's official antipollution symbol. Woodsy Owl wants everyone to "give a hoot" about—

- Clean water and air
- Litter
- Energy conservation
- Recycling, reusing, and reducing trash
- Noise pollution
- Keeping nature beautiful

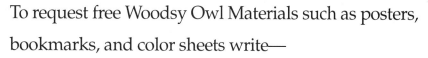

To request free Woodsy Owl Materials such as posters, bookmarks, and color sheets write—

Woodsy Owl Fan Club

P.O. Box 1963

Washington, DC 20250

DO SOMETHING ABOUT LITTER AND POLLUTION

Here are some ways that all of us can help our world.

Remember: Children learn by watching adult role models.

IDEAS

Talk First Then Act

1. Explain to the children that a litterbug is a person who throws trash on the ground or in the water instead of in a trash can.

2. Decide together that your family or class will **never** litter the earth, air, or water.

3. Try to leave each place you go better than you found it by cleaning up after less thoughtful people. When you take a walk or visit a park, tuck a bag in your pocket so you will have a place to put the litter you may find. (Adults will have to ADVISE CHILDREN NOT TO PICK UP GLASS because of the danger of getting cut and GUIDE THEM IN DECIDING WHEN IT IS AND ISN'T APPROPRIATE TO PICK UP LITTER.)

Play "Sort the Litter"

This game is a great way to increase awareness, and children enjoy doing it too.

Natural litter

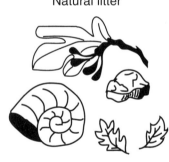

Did you know that such things as leaves, rocks, seed pods, and empty snail shells are called **natural litter?** There are many interesting examples of natural litter lying on the ground waiting to be collected. (See Exploring, page 9, and Thoughtful Collecting, page 15.)

I am sure you know what person-made litter looks like.

You Need:

1. Natural litter
2. Person-made litter

How To:

1. Use any sheet of paper or cardboard that measures at least 12 by 18 inches to make the game board.
2. Draw a line to divide the natural and person-made sides.

Natural   Person-made

3. Print the words and make the faces. (Even very young children can draw the faces.)

4. Now take a walk in your neighborhood, in the park, or in the woods and collect both kinds of litter to use in the game. Put both kinds of litter in the same bag. Why not invite your friends to help you collect?

5. Sit down on the floor with your game board and a sheet of newspaper or something on which you can dump out your collection of litter.

6. As you work together to place the collected items on the proper sides of the board, talk about how the natural items are often interesting and do not spoil the looks of our world while the person-made litter makes our world look messy and awful. ***Be sure to mention we must all take care of our world and never litter.***

REMEMBER TO REMIND THE CHILDREN TO WASH THEIR HANDS THOROUGHLY AFTER HANDLING ANY LITTER.

Another way to play this game is for the adult to have the game board and the collection of litter ready ahead of time. After the children have helped to sort the adult's collection onto the game board, it is fun to take a walk with the children to add more items or to let them make their own collection and game board. I keep this game ready to pull out as a way to start a conversation with children about the huge litter problem we have in our world. (Laminating your game board will keep it in good condition.)

How Long Will Litter Last?

Talk about this list, which is on display at some United States national parks.

Continued.

How Long Will Litter Last?

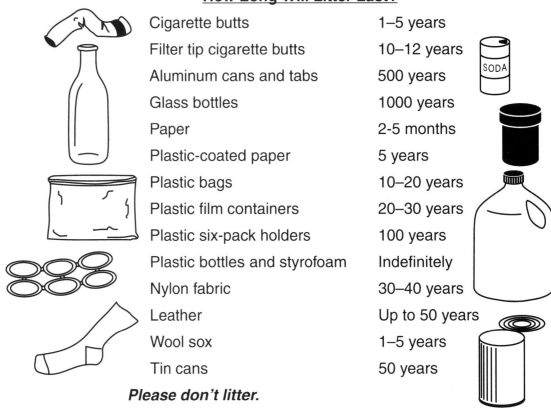

Cigarette butts	1–5 years
Filter tip cigarette butts	10–12 years
Aluminum cans and tabs	500 years
Glass bottles	1000 years
Paper	2-5 months
Plastic-coated paper	5 years
Plastic bags	10–20 years
Plastic film containers	20–30 years
Plastic six-pack holders	100 years
Plastic bottles and styrofoam	Indefinitely
Nylon fabric	30–40 years
Leather	Up to 50 years
Wool sox	1–5 years
Tin cans	50 years

Please don't litter.

Spread the Word

Tell friends about this surprising list. Send a copy to your town or school newspaper.

Make a Display for Your School or Public Library

Glue some of the real items on the list onto a piece of poster board.

Put a copy of the whole list on your display board.

You can put some cigarette butts in a small baggie, fold the bag over, staple it shut, and put it up next to your display with a sign saying, "Remember cigarette butts are litter too."

You can make a difference. After people see your display and read the list, surely they will think twice before littering.

Let's Pretend: Conversation Starters

Talk about the following situations with the children, decide what you would do, and make up more situations.

1. You are eating a banana on your way to a friend's house. Where will you put the skin?

2. You have finished your popcorn and soda at the movie theatre. Where will you put the containers?

3. Your family or class is having a picnic near a beautiful river. After lunch you realize there is no trash can nearby. What will you do with the trash from your picnic?

Seeing Is Believing

Be sure to try this dramatic demonstration. The children and adults act out a picnic near the river.

You Need:

1. A clear plastic storage box (shoebox size) half full of water

2. A few chicken bones and orange peels

3. A crushed soda can and a cup of strong coffee

4. A plastic duck to float in the "river" (optional)

How To (Everything in the list below is pretend except the "river" in number 4 and food in 11):

1. Decide to take a picnic "lunch" and go to the "river."

2. Get in your "car," put on your "seat belts," and "go."

3. Arrive and "play ball," "go fishing," etc.

4. Get hungry and sit in a circle by the "river" (your plastic box with water and plastic duck in it) and pass around your delicious "food"—"chicken," "oranges," "soda" (a special treat), "coffee" for the adults, and "brownies" for dessert.

Continued.

5. Enjoy the "lunch" and comment on the beautiful place, what fun you have had, and how much you appreciate our wonderful world.

6. Decide it is time to go home.

7. Realize there is no trash can nearby.

8. Discuss together what to do with the "trash."

9. Listen to the children's suggestions.

10. Tell the children it is sad but true that some people put trash, oil, and all kinds of waste in our rivers, lakes, ponds, and oceans.

11. Put the real chicken bones, orange peels, soda can, and coffee in the "river" (the plastic box).

12. Talk about—Is it still a beautiful place? What happens to fish and all living things in polluted water?

13. Decide together that **everyone must help care for our world.**

Don't forget to talk about *air pollution* and *noise pollution.* Many people are being harmed by breathing polluted air and permanently damaging their hearing by listening to music and other sounds that are too loud.

DO SOMETHING TO CONSERVE WATER

FACTS

- People are still using the same water the dinosaurs used.

- Water is too precious to waste or pollute.

- The demand for water has increased greatly because of population growth and industrial use throughout the world.

- Gallons of water used: dishwasher, 25 gallons per load; washing machine, 20 gallons per load; shower, 7 to 9 gallons per minute; toilet, 5 to 7 gallons per flush.

What Can You Do?

1. Have a family or class meeting to think of ways to conserve water.

2. Check to see if you are a "water waster."

   A. Does the water run the entire time while you brush your teeth?

   B. Do you take long, long showers?

   C. Do you run the washer and dishwasher with only partial loads?

   If you answered yes, please change these habits to conserve water.

3. Be sure to repair leaky faucets and toilets.

4. Water your lawn without wasteful run-off.

5. Think of more ways to conserve water.

IDEA

Try an Experiment: Find Out If It Takes More Water to Take a Shower or a Bath

How To:

1. Take a bath and fill the tub as high as you usually do. Measure it with a yard stick or a broom handle. Mark that line B for bath.

Continued.

2. Another day take a shower in the same tub. Put the plug in before you shower and measure the water height when you finish. Mark this line S for shower.

Now you will know how to save **water** and the **energy** the water heater uses to heat more water. 😊

DO SOMETHING TO PREVENT FOREST FIRES

Learn more about Smokey Bear and fire safety. Many children know about and love Smokey Bear, the U.S. Forest Service's symbol, who says, "Only you can prevent forest fires." Many years ago the idea for Smokey Bear came from a bear cub who survived a terrible forest fire in New Mexico. This bear lived for many years in the zoo in Washington, D.C.; the bear died in 1975. Smokey wants people to *enjoy but not destroy our beautiful forests.*

Some forest fires are started by lightning, but many forest fires start because of people who are careless with matches, cigarettes, and campfires. Forest fires kill much more than trees and plants. Many animals die in the fire, and many more starve later because their food has been burned and their water is polluted.

IDEA

Build a Make-Believe Campfire Using Smokey Bear's Rules

This is fun to do and helps people of all ages learn and remember important fire safety rules.

You Need:

1. A small garden trowel
2. A small bucket or gallon ice cream tub with a handle (This will hold your pretend sand, dirt, or water for putting out the fire.)
3. 5 or 6 already burned large safety matches in a small zipper bag
4. 5 single sheets of crumpled newspaper (pretend they are pine needles)
5. "Kindling": 8 to 10 small tree branches (fat twigs) that are 8 to 10 inches long
6. "Logs": 8 to 10 large chunks of bark (you sometimes find these lying on the forest floor near dead trees) or you can use fatter twigs. The "log" pieces should be 12 to 14 inches long.

How To (see note below):

Pretend to:

1. Gather your make-believe gear as you prepare for your backpacking adventure. Talk about taking only light weight, necessary things. Don't forget water, rain wear, food, and a flashlight.

NOTE: When I do this activity with a class of children, I have the fire-making materials ready in a box. (If you have a woods nearby, let the children help gather the materials.) After we act out steps 1 through 3 under Pretend To, I have the children sit in a circle around the campfire site. I pass out all the materials, telling the children, "You have make-believe pine needles," or "You have kindling," or "You have logs." I send one child to pretend to fill the bucket and have one child dig the pretend hole. After we check for wind and overhaging trees, we build our campfire, placing the "pine needles" in the "hole" first, followed by the kindling, and then the logs.

Continued.

2. Put on your sturdy hiking boots and drive to the forest. Don't forget to put on your seat belts!

3. Put on your back packs and begin your long hike. Comment on all the wonderful things you see in the forest. Notice the sun is going down and you need to camp for the night.

4. Build your campfire:

   RULE 1 Look for a flat campsite away from overhanging trees. Gather your pine needles, kindling, and logs from the forest.

   RULE 2 Check for wind (no campfires allowed on a windy day).

   RULE 3 Fill up your bucket with sand, water, or dirt (for putting out the fire later).

   RULE 4 Dig a shallow hole with your trowel. (You will build the campfire in the hole.)

   RULE 5 Brush all dry leaves and grass away from the campfire site.

   RULE 6 Build the fire by putting the pine needles in the hole, placing kindling over the needles in the shape of a teepee, and placing the logs over the kindling in the shape of a teepee.

   RULE 7 The adult pretends to strike the match to start the fire and throws the match into the fire.

   Remember: Smokey says, "Many forest fires are started because of careless use of matches and cigarettes."
   NEVER LEAVE A CAMPFIRE UNATTENDED.

5. Roast hot dogs; pass out dried apples and carrot sticks; mix up dried milk.

6. Make smores (a delicious treat) by layering the ingredients in this order: graham cracker, chocolate bar square, roasted marshmallow, more chocolate (optional), graham cracker. Yum, yum! Everyone will want some more (smore).

7. Lie back and look at the stars and moon. Listen for night sounds—owls, coyotes, and wolves—and be glad you understand that they won't bother you. (See What About Owls, page 85, and What About Wolves, page 74.)

8. Put out your campfire with the contents of your bucket. Get into your sleeping bags. You have had an exciting, busy day.

9. The next morning after breakfast be sure your campfire is completely out before you leave the campsite. (The adult should even touch what remains of the campfire to be sure it is cool.) Leave the campsite even cleaner than you found it by taking all trash with you.

10. Remind the children that—
    SMOKEY'S FRIENDS DON'T PLAY WITH MATCHES!

This activity offers endless opportunities for children and adults to talk about the many ways we can all help to take care of our world. Follow-up ideas such as campfire songs and stories are fun. I hope you try it.

To request Smokey Bear Material, write—

U.S. Forest Service

U.S. Department of Agriculture

Auditor's Building

201 14th Street SW

Washington, DC 20250

Some national and state parks have Smokey items such as posters, bookmarks, and color sheets to give to children.

DO SOMETHING ABOUT OUR TRASH PROBLEM: RECYCLE—REDUCE—REUSE—REACT

The United States of America is in a mess. Our beautiful country is being buried by trash. For too long America has been a throw-away society. **Conservation** *means wise* *use,* and now is the time for everyone to help by practicing the 4 R's—*r*ecycle, *r*educe, *r*euse, *r*eact. Let's learn how.

Recycle

Recycling is a great family project. Even very young children can help.

- The United States produces huge amounts of solid waste (garbage and trash), which most of us just call **trash.**

- Our landfills are filling up fast. (See page 156.)

- The United States is the largest consumer of paper in the world.

- If everyone in the United States recycled their Sunday newspapers, we would save 500,000 trees every week.

- Each year we throw away 28 billion glass bottles and jars.

- Each hour we empty 2.5 million plastic bottles.

- We use over 65 billion aluminum cans every week.

So let's all pitch in and recycle.

IDEAS

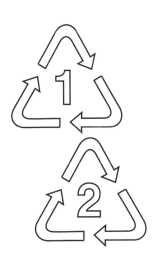

How To Become Recyclers

1. Explain to the children that recycling means taking something "old" and making it into something new that can be used again.

2. Some communities offer curbside recycling pickups. Check with your city hall about the location of recycling centers and also look up recycling centers in the phone book.

3. Visit a center near you to see which items it accepts. Many centers accept newspaper, aluminum cans, clear, green, and brown glass, plastic milk jugs, two-liter soda bottles, and other plastic containers marked 1 or 2 within the special recycle symbol stamped into the plastic on the bottom of many plastic containers. Some centers accept steel cans, motor oil, corrugated cardboard, scrap metal, and plastic containers marked with other numbers within the symbol. Some centers pay money for certain items.

4. Have a family meeting to decide how your family can work together to help our world by recycling as many items as possible yourselves, perhaps by—

   - Spreading the word about recycling to neighbors and friends
   - Offering to take recyclable materials to the depository for elderly people who might need help with this job
   - Saving the money you may make recycling for a special family purchase or event or to give to a favorite charity.

   The possibilities for fun and good works are endless.

5. Begin to save and separate items for recycling. (Rinse out cans and bottles to avoid rodents and insects. Labels do not need to be soaked off jars.)

6. Be proud to be recyclers!

Continued.

Sing Recycle Songs

Song 1 Tune: *I'm a Little Teapot*

We should all recycle—I hope you do.
Newspaper and glass, to name just a few.
Aluminum will even earn money for you.
Ask your neighbors to recycle, too.
Hooray for recycling!

Song 2 Tune: *The More We Get Together*

The more we all recycle, recycle, recycle
The more we all recycle
The happier we'll be.
Cause your world is my world
And my world is your world.
The more we all recycle, the happier we'll be!

It is fun to jump up as high as you can and shout "Hooray for recycling!"

Reduce and Reuse

LET'S FIND OUT MORE ABOUT LANDFILLS

Biodegradable

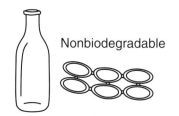

Nonbiodegradable

In landfills layers of trash are smashed down and covered with dirt. More and more layers are added, and the landfill becomes nearly airtight and dry. Did you know that scientists called "garbologists" have taken deep core samples of trash that has been buried in landfills for many years? Before we talk about their discoveries, let me explain that when you bury items that were once alive (like paper which is made from trees), they will rot away (**decompose**) and enrich the soil. Scientists call such items **biodegradable.** Items made of glass and plastic will not rot away. These items are said to be **nonbiodegradable.**

By studying the samples of the long-buried trash these scientists now know that even newspaper and other biodegradable items do *not* rot away when buried in a landfill. For example, they found an ear of corn that had been buried for 20 years near a newspaper dated 20 years ago that was still readable!

Now that we know that even biodegradable items do not rot away in landfills, and since our landfill space will soon be gone, let's all *recycle* as much as we can and also learn to *reduce, reuse,* and *react.*

IDEAS

Bury Some Trash and See What Happens

It is great fun and very interesting to try this idea, but *remember,* conditions are very different in your yard than in a landfill. In your yard, air, water, and nature's decomposers such as earthworms, sowbugs, millipedes, and  fungus are at work. You and the children will be amazed at the results when you dig up the trash!

How To:

1. In a mesh onion bag place a paper napkin, tea bag, apple core, leaves, small glass object, small plastic items like a plastic spoon or straw. Make a list of these items.

2. Write the date on your list before you bury the bag in a marked spot in your yard. Dig it up 6 months later to see *what happened.* Check your list to see what is missing.

Continued.

Decide to Reduce the Amount of Trash You Produce

How To:

Follow these simple tips and think up more. Check off the ideas you pledge to do.

1. Don't waste paper. Use both sides. Use junk mail as scratch paper. Use a dish cloth instead of a paper towel for wiping up spills. Use cloth instead of paper napkins. (See below for a fun way to make free napkin rings.)

2. Buy only what you need. Buy products with the least amount of packaging. Buy the larger size or in bulk when possible.

3. Buy recycled paper products or products packaged in recycled or recyclable paper. ***Don't be fooled:*** All recycled paper products are not equal. Look for and buy **postconsumer** recycled paper. This is made from new paper pulp and paper recycled by people at home or at the office. **Preconsumer** recycled paper has been in use for many years and is made of new paper pulp and scraps of paper from paper manufacturers or printers.

4. Buy good quality things that will last and can be repaired.

5. Avoid using throw-aways such as paper and plastic plates and cups, disposable diapers, and razors.

Make Your Own Napkin Rings

You will love using real napkins. Buy the kind that wash easily with no ironing required. You will save money, since you won't need to buy paper napkins, and you will also reduce trash in the landfills! Each member of the family will need a napkin ring, and they must all be different.

You Need:

1. Empty toilet paper or paper towel roll
2. Ruler
3. Pencil
4. Markers, crayons, or yarn

How To:

1. Take an empty toilet paper or paper towel roll and mark off 1- to 1 1/2-inch rings with a pencil.

2. Smash it down a little so you can cut the sections off to make your rings. This can be done with a paper cutter if one is available. (USING THE PAPER CUTTER IS AN ADULT OR OLDER CHILD JOB. Cutting by hand may be a child or adult job depending on the child's scissor skills.)

3. Everyone can decorate his or her own napkin ring, or a child may want to make one for every family member or for gifts for grandma and grandpa or a teacher. Make everyone's different. Markers or crayon may be used to draw the decorations.

4. You might want to wrap some rings in different colored yarn scraps:

   a. Tie the yarn onto the ring. Make a knot leaving a long enough end so you can make another knot later.

   b. Wrap the yarn around and around the ring until the ring is covered with yarn.

   c. Knot again using the end you left in step *a* and the end left after wrapping.

   d. Tuck in the ends, and you have a nice napkin ring.

Begin to Reuse As Many Things As Possible

How To:

1. Take bags to the store when you shop and don't accept extra bags.

2. Save wrapping paper and ribbon to use again.

3. Think of ways to reuse packaging materials, boxes, and containers of all kinds.

4. Take extra hangers back to the cleaners.

5. Give unneeded clothing, appliances, and so on to someone else.

Continued.

6. Reuse lunch bags or buy a reusable lunch box or bag.

7. Save aluminum foil, plastic, and paper bags to use again.

8. Compost your kitchen and yard waste.

Composting

In nature, leaves fall into the woods each year. No one rakes them up. They slowly rot away, making wonderful spongy topsoil that holds moisture and gives new tree seedlings a perfect place to sprout and grow. That is nature's composting process. The word **compost** means a mixture of any material that used to be alive (organic material) that has rotted away (decomposed). Compost is great. It can be used as a mulch or, when mixed in dirt, will "lighten up" the soil and help it hold water. Anyone who has a yard can compost, and it doesn't have to be a big job. (Also see Compost with Earthworms in Your Home or Classroom, page 68.)

Don't let complicated composting rules scare you. There is really no wrong way to compost except it is important to follow the do's and don'ts. It feels so good to know you are *reusing* leaves (as nature does) and kitchen waste instead of dumping these good things into a landfill to sit forever.

You need leaves, grass and plant clippings, and soil, which will contain the earthworms, bacteria, millipedes and other **decomposers** that make the process work.

Kitchen wastes are great for your compost pile.

Here are the do's and don'ts:

- *Do add* any vegetable or fruit peelings, seeds, rinds, coffee grounds, tea leaves, crushed egg shells.

- *Don't add* butter, oleo, cheese, milk or cream, meat, fish, mayonnaise, peanut butter, or vegetable oil. Pet feces should not be added because they may contain harmful organisms.

You won't attract animals (such as rats, mice, dogs, cats, raccoons) if you follow these do's and don'ts.

This means you won't scrape left overs such as buttered vegetables, spaghetti, or a half eaten sandwich into your compost containers.

I leave a plastic ice cream carton with a tight fitting lid in my kitchen sink for collecting my kitchen scraps, yellow leaves off my house plants, and lint from my clothes dryer, which will all go into my compost pile.

Chopping up banana peels and rinds makes them decompose faster, so I use my kitchen scissors and quickly chop them up as I add them to my carton when time allows.

My family bought a leaf grinding machine; some people chop up leaves with the lawn mower, but it is not necessary to do either of these things. Smaller pieces will just rot away more quickly.

How I Compost:

Last summer I decided to compost, but I didn't know much about it. I had a pile of leaves, some grass clippings, and my kitchen waste. Behind my garage I dug a hole about 6 inches deep, dumped in my garbage, a shovel full of leaves and some grass clipping, chopped these together a bit with my shovel and covered it over with soil. Each time I had a carton of waste, I repeated this process. I kept the area moist but not soggy. After a while I noticed a big difference in my soil (which was clay) back there. I have mixed the compost in with regular soil in garden areas.

A friend started her compost pile by wetting down (moist but not soggy) a pile of leaves in the corner of her yard. She mixes in soil, yard clippings, kitchen waste, more leaves, soil. She and I are both surprised by how the pile goes down quickly as these things all decompose.

My purpose here is to encourage you to begin by letting you know that composting does not have to be a complicated, exact process. You can get information about composting from your city hall or from your state natural resources department.

React

Ways we can make a difference: (1) Refuse to buy products that are harmful to the environment. (2) Save energy by turning off lights and TV when they are not in use and by wearing a sweater instead of turning up the heat. (3) Use phosphate-free detergent and borax or washing soda instead of chlorine bleach. (4) Use vinegar and baking soda in place of cleanser (see page 163 for a fun idea). (5) Buy food and drinks in containers that can be recycled. (6) Buy rechargeable batteries and a battery recharger. (7) Write and call store owners and manufacturers (many companies put addresses and phone numbers on the package) to let them know you won't buy overpackaged, nonrecyclable packaging or products harmful to the environment. (8) Encourage other people to recycle, reduce, reuse, and react!

IDEAS

Make a Game of Reducing Lunch-time Trash

Grownups and children can play this Reuse Game.

You Need:

1. A cloth (reuseable) lunch bag or lunch box
2. A small thermos
3. A cloth napkin

4. A reuseable fork and spoon

5. Washable food containers to hold your sandwich, fruit, or yogurt

6. Reuseable baggies for snacks and cookies

How To:

1. The adult must provide the necessary reuseable items mentioned above in How To.

2. Take the little extra time it takes to fill and then wash the reuseable containers, or better still, make packing lunch a shared parent and child job.

   The child must—

   1. Understand why making less or no trash is important.

   2. Be responsible for bringing home the reuseable lunch items each day (even the baggies).

 If the children get excited about helping our world, they will think of more good ideas for you to try.

Make Vinegar–Baking Soda Cleanser

  We should avoid chlorine cleansers because chlorine and phosphates cause problems in our water systems. Vinegar and baking soda are great natural cleaners, and they do not harm the water system.

   Children enjoy doing this, and it's fun to see the fizz (a chemical reaction) when the vinegar and baking soda get together.

How To:

Let the children help.

1. Put baking soda in shaker can or jar. You can make a container by poking nail holes in a small plastic yogurt carton.

2. Put vinegar (any kind will do) in a spray bottle.

3. Label these two containers.

Continued.

4. Spray vinegar in the sink; sprinkle baking soda on the vinegar; enjoy the fizzy action; wipe the sink clean with a rag or sponge.

This works well, is fun, and helps our world.

Write Letters—Make Phone Calls—Let Children Help You Make Your Views Known

Consumer views are important to manufacturers, store owners, and government officials. If you and your children feel strongly about helping our world in the various ways we have talked about in this chapter, *please take a little extra time to make your views known.* You can make a positive difference.

How To:

1. During a family conversation you might decide to *react* about a certain issue. Perhaps you will decide to write a manufacturing firm (such as a toy or food company) that overpackages its products or does not package in recyclable containers. An address and sometimes an 800 phone number are on the package.

2. Even young children can be included in deciding what to say. They can put on the stamp and go along to mail the letter. Older children can actually write the letter.

3. Write in your Science Record Notebook who you wrote, what it was about, and the date you mailed the letter.

4. Wait until all family members are together before opening and reading the reply.

5. Share with others the result of your making your views known.

BE A CONSERVATIONIST

Conservationists care about our world. They—

- Faithfully recycle, reduce, reuse, and react.
- Never litter or pollute and try to leave the world better than they found it.
- Love to look at wildflowers but never pick them.
- Appreciate the wild creatures in our world.
- Know it is important to plant trees and gardens.
- Try to learn new ways to help our world.

People of all ages can make a difference. Won't you join the conservationists today?

Our world needs lots of love and tender care. So—Won't you tell all your neighbors and all your kin, it really helps our world when we all pitch in!

SUGGESTED READINGS

Cherry, Lynne. *The Great Kapok Tree.* A Gulliver Book. New York: Harcourt Brace Jovanovich, 1990.

Chief Seattle. *Brother Eagle, Sister Sky: A Message from Chief Seattle.* New York: Dial Books, 1991.

Dr. Seuss. *The Lorax.* New York: Random House, 1971.

Van Allsburg, Chris. *Just a Dream.* Boston: Houghton Mifflin Co., 1990.

Chapter 9
Fitness, Food, and Fun

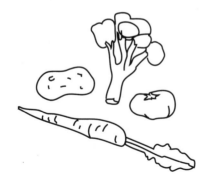

Remember that your children are watching all you do.
They notice how you eat and act—they want to be like you.

Helping children establish good health habits *early* in their lives is so important!

Experts believe that the life-style behaviors we establish early usually carry over into adulthood. If a child's diet includes lots of junk food, if he or she spends hours watching television, or if the child does not take part in vigorous physical activity on a regular basis, experts believe that long-range health problems are almost a certainty.

Give your children an important gift: Help them learn to enjoy healthy foods and an active life-style.

Because of the health information that is now available, many adults are examining their own health habits as well as being concerned about the health habits of their children.

Remember: Set a good example—your children are learning from you.

WE ARE WHAT WE EAT

FACTS

- The number one killer in America today is *heart disease.*

- High blood cholesterol is linked to increased risk of heart disease.

- **SOME CHILDREN HAVE HIGH BLOOD CHOLESTEROL LEVELS AND HIGH BLOOD PRESSURE.**

- The first line of defense against high blood cholesterol is a low-fat, low-cholesterol diet.

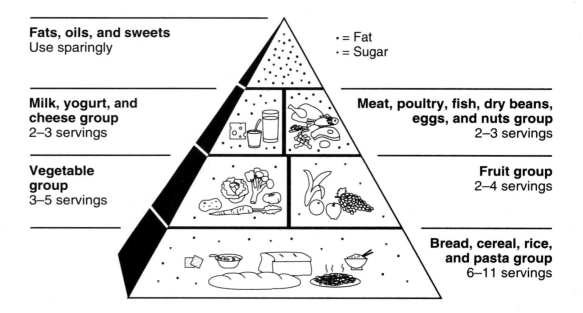

In 1992 the U.S. Department of Agriculture introduced the Food Guide Pyramid. It is a new look for the old four food groups. The pyramid shows clearly that fats, oils, and sweets should be eaten sparingly. To receive the brochure called Food Guide Pyramid: A Guide to Daily Food Choices, send $1.00 to:

Consumer Information Center

Department 159-Y

Pueblo, CO 81009

The American Heart Association, the American Cancer Society and the National Dairy Council offer excellent nutrition information and materials designed especially for children. See Health Hazards, page 176, to learn how to contact these organizations.

IDEAS

Learn to Read Those Labels

By reading the label we can better understand what we are buying. Did you know that every ingredient in each product we buy must be listed on the package under Ingredients? The major ingredient (by weight) must be listed first, followed by the other ingredients, which are listed in order by weight—from the greatest to the least.

For example, sugar is used in products under many different names such as sucrose, glucose, dextrose, honey, corn syrup, lactose, and maltose. So—if you see one of these sugars listed as one of the first three ingredients or if several sugars are listed on the label, the product is probably high in sugar.

CHOCO CHUMS

Sugar-Coated Puff Balls

When reading labels you should also know that ***5 g (grams) of sugar = 1 teaspoon of sugar.*** Many processed cereal products are very high in sugar content in contrast to such products as rolled oats and cream of wheat, which have no added sugar. Help children understand how much "hidden" sugar is in each product and then make a family decision about how much sugar is too much sugar.

Also watch out for high levels of fat and salt.

Become Sodium Smart

FACTS

- Some sodium is needed by our bodies.
- Most Americans consume far more sodium than they need.
- Most sodium in the American diet comes from table salt.

Continued.

- Sodium is found naturally in some foods and is added to many foods and drinks.
- Most sodium is added to processed foods to keep them from spoiling or to flavor them.
- There are many sodium-containing ingredients. Baking powder, baking soda, sodium saccharin, and sodium citrate are just a few.
- Reducing sodium intake may help people avoid high blood pressure, which can lead to heart disease and stroke.

The more processed a food, the more sodium it contains. Here are a few surprises!

1 small fresh tomato has 10 milligrams (mg) salt	1/2 cup tomato juice has 440 mg salt	1/2 cup of tomato sauce has 741 mg salt
1/2 cup of fresh peas has 2 mg salt	1/2 cup of canned peas has 186 mg salt	1 cup of pea soup has 987 mg salt
3 ounces of pork has 59 mg salt	4 slices of bacon has 404 mg salt	3 ounces of ham has 1009 mg salt

Learn More About Fat—Fat—Fat

Remember some children have high blood cholesterol and high blood pressure.

Eating a diet high in fat causes high blood cholesterol levels in many people. High blood cholesterol levels increase the risk of heart disease.

Fats are said to be either saturated or unsaturated. A small amount of fat is needed by our bodies, but beware of the saturated fats.

This chart (a partial list) is helpful in seeing the difference:

Ingredients high in saturated fatty acids		Ingredients (oils) high in unsaturated fatty acids	
Beef fat	Cream	Corn	Sesame
Butter	Lard	Cottonseed	Soybean
Cocoa butter	Palm oil	Safflower	Sunflower
Coconut oil			

Remember to:

- Avoid too much total fat, go easy on products listing a fat or oil first, or listing many fat and oil ingredients on their label.
- Use the chart above to help you identify some of the many different sources of fats.

Tips on How to Avoid Too Much Fat, Saturated Fat, and Cholesterol

1. Choose lean cuts of meat; trim fat from the meat before and/or after cooking.
2. Remove the skin from poultry before cooking.
3. Roast, bake, broil, or simmer meat, poultry, or fish.
4. Steam, boil, or bake vegetables or, for a change, stirfry in a small amount of vegetable oil.
5. Enjoy vegetables plain or season them with herbs and spices rather than with sauces, butter, or margarine.
6. Use low fat dairy products. Use margarine instead of butter.
7. When possible, use oil instead of shortening in baked products.

Good news! When you lower your fat intake you also take in fewer calories (1 tablespoon of fat equals 100 calories) without reducing good nutrition!

Since experts advise us to keep our weight within the recommended range, this is very good news.

Beware of Packaging Gimmicks

Experts warn that while manufacturers often do a good job of making their product appeal to children by using bright colors and cartoon characters on their packaging, many do a poor job of including nutritious ingredients in their food.

For example:

- Some frozen dinners packaged to appeal to children contain very high amounts of salt and fat.
- Many cereal products are very high in sugar.

You can make a difference. Write to the manufacturers or call them on their 1-800 phone numbers to complain about the high fat, salt, and sugar content in many of the foods produced especially to appeal to children. Tell the manufacturers about your objection and that you won't buy the product until the problem is corrected. They will probably write to you and take steps to improve the quality of the product.

Be sure to let the children take an active part in calling or writing the letter to the manufacturer.

Learn More About Healthy Snacks

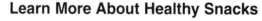

Eat More	Eat Less
Fresh fruits and vegetables	Packaged fruit roll ups
Unsalted nuts and popcorn	Potato and other snack chips
Peanut butter and crackers, whole grain bread, graham crackers	White bread, sweet rolls, doughnuts, cookies
Low-fat milk and natural fruit juice	Whole and chocolate milk and soda pop

Special Occasion Foods to use sparingly include fried foods, like french fries and fried chicken, most foods at fast food restaurants, candy, cake, ice cream, soda pop, salty snacks, and other sweets.

Keeping Score—What You Eat Day By Day

Monday, October 2, 1993		
Milk	Grain	Meat
ᄔᄔ	IIII	II
Fruits + Veggies	Snacks	Special Treats
III	II	I

On a chalk board or paper the children will help you keep a record of the foods your family eats.

When you record snacks and special treats in special columns, it helps everyone see the kinds of snack foods you use and how often you have special treats.

Don't Forget the Water!

Drink 6 to 8 glasses a day in addition to other liquids.

Don't Forget to Visit Your Dentist Regularly!

Brush and floss your way to a healthy smile.

Fun With the Five Food Groups

(You will learn about the Food Groups in the Food Guide Pyramid on page 168.)

Children enjoy making food group posters.

You Need:

The Food Pyramid picture

How To (this is an individual, family, or class project):

1. Look for pictures of foods in colorful grocery ads or magazines.
2. Cut them out and glue them on paper to make your posters.
3. Look over the recipes in the section called Yummy in the Tummy, page 179, to see where the ingredients fit in the Food Pyramid. Maybe you will want to buy some of the ingredients needed to make these nutritious, yummy foods.

Continued.

A Grocery Store Adventure

Take the children to the grocery store* to:

1. Read those labels—see what is really in the cereals, crackers, fruit roll ups, etc. you usually buy!

2. Consider trying—oat bran, rolled oats, and other hot cereals (yummy plain or with raisins).

3. Explore the produce section and buy some fresh fruits and vegetables you have never tasted!

4. Have a tasting party and try your newly-found foods— perhaps with a healthy dip. (See Mock Sour Cream, page 181.)

*If it isn't possible to take the children to the store with you, bring some food home so you can try these ideas.

EXERCISE FOR GOOD HEALTH— FEEL BETTER, LOOK BETTER, WORK AND PLAY BETTER

Some experts feel it is as important for children to take part in regular vigorous exercise as it is to learn to read and do math.

Everyone has heard that "exercise is good for you," but most Americans of all ages get little vigorous exercise at work, school, play or during leisure hours.

Many children spend long hours watching television or playing video games. These activities may offer some benefits but lack opportunity for active involvement and take the time that could be spent in active play.

Authorities on fitness say:

- Both proper nutrition and regular exercise are necessary for maximum fitness.

- Many children do not play outdoors enough or receive proper instruction in exercise and nutrition at school.

- It is best to build healthy life-style habits early because early habits usually carry over into adulthood.

- Children whose parents are involved in regular physical activity are more likely to enjoy physical activity themselves, both as children and as they become adults.

- For adults the American Health Association suggests this exercise prescription for your health—Exercise briskly at least 30–60 minutes 3–4 times per week.

IDEAS

Consider a Plan of Action—What Can You Do?

1. Encourage your children to run, play, ride bikes, swim, walk, climb on climbers, swing—move their bodies.
2. Enjoy family activities that provide regular physical activity— perhaps brisk walking, biking, swimming, jumping rope, or hiking.
3. Check with your school to be sure an appropriate, regular, vigorous exercise program is part of each child's school day.

Walk Your Way to Good Health

Why not plan to take family walks on a regular schedule— perhaps daily or 3 times a week. Begin with short walks and slowly build up your distance. Try walking at a brisk pace but with young children, expect frequent stops for exploring and resting. Keep track of your "miles walked" on your Science Calendar or in your Science Record Book.

Continued.

Plan a party to celebrate walking 10 miles or a distance goal your family sets.

Hiking Is Fun for All Ages!
Contact: Your county, state and national parks for information on marked hiking trails.

Remember: While hiking watch for animal tracks in the mud or snow.

HEALTH HAZARDS—WHAT CAN WE DO?

We must face the fact that even young children are exposed to smoking, alcohol, and drugs and that many children of all ages are poorly nourished and lack adequate exercise. Children need age-appropriate information about all these health hazards at a very early age.

Good news! Interesting, meaningful, often free materials that are especially designed for children are available to help provide this information.

IDEA

Call for Help
The following organizations are hoping you will call.

The American Cancer Society provides free curriculum materials for teachers as well as audio visuals and other teaching aids for ages preschool through twelfth grade. The Huffless, Puffless Dragon is the character features in their early childhood curriculum materials. Spider Man and Health Man appear in the elementary curriculum. Eat Smart is their nutritional program providing information for all ages.

For information contact your local American Cancer Society office or call 1-800-ACS-2345.

The American Heart Association provides free curriculum materials for teachers and has schoolsite programs dedicated to encouraging students from preschool through twelfth grade to develop heart healthy habits. The Heart Treasure Chest is a hands-on teaching tool developed for use with 3 to 5 year-olds; the Getting to Know Your Heart program is designed for grades 1 through 6; Heart Decisions is a program to teach older children the relationships between life-styles and health.

For information contact your local American Heart Association office or call 1-800-AHA-USA1.

Chef Combo

The National Dairy Council offers nutrition education materials, audio visuals, posters, and brochures for preschool through adulthood. Chef Combo, their nutrition education puppet, provides experiences that encourage wise food choices by three to six year olds. Their Super You and Body Walk programs combine the importance of both nutrition and physical activity.

Dairy Council materials are sometimes free and sometimes low cost.

For information contact you local Dairy Council office or write
National Dairy Council
O'Hare International Center, Suite 900
10255 West Higgins Road
Rosemont, IL 60018-5616
Phone 708-803-2000   Fax 708-803-2077

The American Lung Association has informational materials on smoking, how to stop smoking, and the effects of second hand smoke on both children and adults. They offer educational materials, posters, brochures, and audio visuals for ages preschool through adulthood.

Continued.

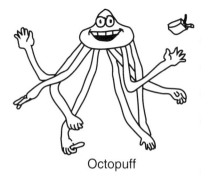

Octopuff

I have used their audio visual called Octopuff in Kumquat with great success with preschool and kindergarten age children. Its educational theme is filled with excitement and is especially created for children four to eight yours old. My students enjoy and learn from Octopuff year after year.

For information contact your local American Lung Association office or write

The American Lung Association National Office

1740 Broadway

New York, NY 10019

NOTE: The Smoke-Free Class of 2000 is a national project and a combined effort of the American Heart Association, the American Cancer Society and the American Lung Association. This 12-year education and awareness project focuses on children who entered first grade in 1988 and will graduate in the year 2000. Contact any of the three agencies mentioned above for information.

D.A.R.E. (Drug Abuse Resistance Education) is a prevention program now being used in many communities throughout the United States. I have personal knowledge of D.A.R.E.'s success in my community, Brentwood, Missouri, where it has been used in our elementary schools since 1987. D.A.R.E. has been well received by the students, parents, and teachers and is now a part of the school curriculum kindergarten through tenth grade. One unique feature of D.A.R.E. is the use of police officers as instructors. D.A.R.E. officers are carefully selected and trained before they are assigned to their classroom beat.

The resistance education focuses on four major areas:

- Providing accurate information about alcohol and drugs
- Teaching students decision-making skills
- Showing them how to resist peer pressure
- Giving them alternatives to drug use

During the weeks of D.A.R.E. instruction, the officer visits school once a week staying on campus all day, interacting with students during lunch and recess as well as presenting a part of the planned instructional material.

For information contact your local police department or call D.A.R.E. America 1-800-223-DARE.

The National Council on Alcoholism and Drug Abuse is available to assist you in a professional and confidential manner with any question or concern related to alcohol and other drug problems. Not all local offices offer the same prevention services. I am familiar with the St. Louis office's prevention programs which include an elementary curriculum called WINNERS and an alcohol/drug free social and recreational activities program call TREND.

For information contact you local NCADA office or call 1-800-475-HOPE.

YUMMY IN THE TUMMY

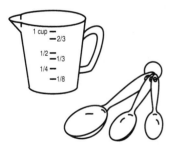

Children enjoy cooking. Preparing food is *fun* and is also important *work.*

Cooking is *science* too—weighing, measuring, combining, dissolving, seeing ingredients change form when combined, heated, or cooled. (The hard apple is soft after cooking.)

Cooking is *teamwork,* and children learn—

- To follow directions in a certain sequence.
- New words and meanings.
- The basic principles of good nutrition.
- The joy of preparing and sharing delicious food.

COOKING WITH CHILDREN— HELPFUL HINTS

1. Use electric appliances such as mixers and blenders as little as possible. Let the children mix, stir, grate, chop, and so on.

2. Decide together what to cook.

3. Teach children to wash their hands before cooking.

4. To keep germs away, decide to taste *only* when it is time to lick the bowl.

5. Provide a work space at child level. Your kitchen table is a better height than a counter top.

6. Cover the work surface with old terry cloth towels or something that can be gathered up, shaken out, and washed.

7. Let the children help you collect the ingredients and name each one.

8. Dump the dry ingredients into a large, flat pan so the children can easily spoon the ingredients into the cup.

9. Teach each child to heap the cup or measuring spoon more than full before leveling it off with a knife.

10. Divide up measuring and stirring jobs and take turns.

11. Allow children to practice cracking eggs (in a separate dish).

12. AVOID ACCIDENTS BY GIVING THE CHILDREN TABLE KNIVES ONLY FOR CHOPPING.

13. Talk about the danger of sharp knives and hot stoves. Explain that some parts of cooking are adult jobs.

14. To wash fruits and vegetables, place a dish pan of clean water on the table.

15. Make cooking with children a pleasure by keeping it simple and not expecting perfection!

ON TO THE RECIPES!

Remember: Let the children do as much as possible.

Abbreviations used: T. = tablespoon; t. = teaspoon.

Here is an American Heart Association suggestion for a low-fat dip.

Mock Sour Cream

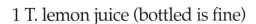

You Need:

2 T. skim milk

1 T. lemon juice (bottled is fine)

1 cup low fat cottage cheese

How To:

Place all ingredients in a blender and mix on medium-high speed until smooth and creamy.

NOTE: This may not "act" like regular sour cream in your recipes that call for sour cream. Experiment with small amounts of ingredients to see if it can be used as a substitute.

Ants on a Log

You Need:

Celery—raisins—fillings such as cheese spread and peanut butter

How To:

1. The children wash and cut celery to 3- or 4-inch pieces.
2. Spread the filling in the celery.
3. Dot it with raisins.
4. Pretend the raisins are ants on a log.

Granola: Nutritious and Fun to Make

We eat this as a breakfast cereal, sometimes mix it with other dry cereals, and often eat it as a spoonable snack.

You Need:

4 cups uncooked old fashioned oatmeal (not quick or instant)

1 cup wheat germ

1 cup grated coconut (see note below)

1 or 2 T. brown sugar

1/3 cup vegetable oil like Puritan or Mazola Oil

1/2 cup honey or light corn syrup

1 T. pure vanilla extract

1 1/2 cups of shelled low-salt sunflower seeds (or a mixture of sesame and sunflower seeds)

1 1/2 cups coarsely broken low-salt peanuts or mixed nuts

NOTE: Coconut is a high-fat food. You may wish to omit it from the recipe. I don't add it.

How To:

Find the combination your family likes.

Measure and mix all dry ingredients in a large bowl. In a sauce pan combine oil, honey, and vanilla and warm. Add this to the dry ingredients and stir until all particles are coated. Spread this mixture out on a long, low rimmed greased baking sheet. A pan 17 by 11 1/2 inches or 13 by 9 1/2 inches will do. Bake for 1 hour at 250 degrees. Turn the mixture with a spoon about every 15 minutes while baking. When cool, add dried fruits such as raisins and store in an air-tight container. (We add raisins as we eat the granola because we think the stored granola stays crisper.)

Mini Pops

You Need:

Fruit juice—apple, orange, grape

How To:

1. Fill small paper cups, plastic pill cups, or an ice cube tray 2/3 full of juice. (Explain to the children that *liquid expands* when it freezes.)

2. Cover the cups or tray with a double thickness of aluminum foil. Crimp all around the edges.

3. Slit the foil in the center of each "pop" and push a popsicle stick in each one.

4. Place carefully in the freezer.

 5. Remove one at a time as needed. Eat outside or in the bath tub.

Food mill

Applesauce—No Peeling—Just Fun and Good

This is one of my favorite projects to do with children. It does require that you have a food mill or cone-type strainer.

Cone-type strainer

I like the food mill better.

I use and recommend you buy a 2 quart size Foley food mill. It also comes in a 3 1/2 quart size, but I prefer the 2 quart. (Other brands may be fine, too.) Food mills may be purchased or ordered in housewares departments or hardware stores. It is a worthwhile investment and lasts forever. You may find one at a garage sale!

Applesauce freezes well (I use plastic cottage cheese cartons) so you can easily make a year's supply at "apple time." *What a great family project.*

You Need:

3 pounds of apples (We like the flavor of jonathan apples for sauce and pies.)

1 1/2 to 2 cups water

Sugar to taste—perhaps 1/3 to 2/3 cup

Cinnamon to sprinkle on at serving time (don't cook with apples)

A large cooking pot and a food mill

How To (Many children can work at one time):

1. Cover the table with terry cloth towels (no need for cutting boards), put a dishpan of water (for washing apples) and table knives on the table. *You do not need to peel or remove stems or seeds. These all stay in the food mill!*

2. Children and adults wash the apples, cut the apple into halves or quarters (see note), put the apples into the cooking pot, add the water. Gather loose seeds for planting (see pages 93 and 96).

NOTE: Cutting apples with table knives takes muscle! Some children will need help; some will work and work on their own; others will be less interested.

As You Work:

Cut one apple across and find the "star."

Put a "star" half on your science shelf and observe the changes.

Talk about how hard the apples are. Wonder together how they will be after cooking.

THE ADULTS cook the apples in a covered pot (stir now and then) until the apples are very soft. (Enjoy the smell as the apples cook.) Gather a few children at a time. KEEP THE HOT PAN AWAY FROM THE CHILDREN.

Hook the food mill onto a large bowl.

Dip some warm apples into the food mill.

Everyone takes turns turning the handle to strain the sauce into the bowl.

Add the sugar while the sauce is warm. Let the children stir it in so they can see the sugar dissolve in the warm applesauce. *Delicious* warm or cool, by itself, or with pork or meat loaf. I hope you try it.

Strawberry-Pineapple Gelatin

You Need:

1 3-ounce package strawberry gelatin

3/4 cup boiling water

1 8-ounce can crushed pineapple—juice and all

1 10-ounce package frozen strawberries—juice and all— thawed

How To:

THE ADULT ADDS THE BOILING WATER to the gelatin.

Talk about the word **dissolve** as the child stirs the water and gelatin together.

Add the pineapple and strawberries, juice and all. (Bananas may be sliced and added too.)

Stir together and put in one or many molds.

Eat a Clown for Lunch! Think of Other Fun Creations

Head: Hard cooked egg (with a bit sliced off one side)

Hat: Green pepper

Hair: Grated carrot or cheese

Eyes and Nose: Raisin bits

Mouth: Cherry or pimento slice

Body: Tomato slice

Ruffles: Fresh parsley

Buttons: Olive or pickle slices

Arms: Celery sticks or small sweet pickles

Legs: Hot dog in a bun - cut in half.

Children love to create and eat this clown.

Vegetable Beef Soup

This is a great family or class project. Class members can bring a vegetable from home and call it **sharing soup.**

You Need:

1 pound or more beef shank

3 carrots

2 large onions

2 large celery stalks with leaves

1/3 cup barley

8-ounce can tomato sauce

4 to 5 cups water

You may add other vegetables of your choice.

How To:

1. THE ADULTS SIMMER the beef shank, tomato sauce, and water in a covered pot for 2 hours.

2. Set up your table covered with towels, a dish pan of water, and table knives as you did under Applesauce, How To step 1 on page 184. *The children can scrub the carrots with a stiff brush—no need to peel the carrots.*

    NOTE: Carrots are very hard to cut with table knives so partially precook the carrots to soften them a bit if cooking with very young children.

3. Everyone works together chopping up the celery and leaves, onions (the results are worth the tears), and carrots. Put all the chopped vegetables into a bowl.

4. THE ADULT ADDS the vegetables and barley to the simmering meat and tomato mixture.

5. Simmer this (covered) 1 or 2 more hours. Stir now and then.

6. THE ADULT REMOVES the beef shanks to cool. Cut the meat into bite-size chunks.

This is wonderful served with english muffins.

Vegetarian Vegetable Soup

How To:

Use V8 juice for the liquid.

Chop and add as many vegetables as you wish (see items 2 and 3 under Vegetable Beef Soup, How To).

 **Lima Bean Soup**

You Need:

1 1/2 pounds large dried lima beans

1 large ham shank (not ham hock)

3 onions

3 celery stalks with leaves

3 carrots

3 T. lemon juice (bottled is fine)

8 ounces canned tomatoes (cut in bite-size chunks)

How To:

1. The night before making the soup, add 6 cups of water to the beans, bring to a boil, and turn off the burner. Add 1 1/2 teaspoons of baking soda and let sit, covered, overnight. (The baking soda may help prevent the gas discomfort associated with beans.)

2. The next day drain the beans and rinse them well.

3. For chopping vegetables follow the directions given in steps 2 and 3 under Vegetable Beef Soup, How To.

4. Put the soaked limas, ham shank, chopped vegetables, tomatoes, and lemon juice in a large cooking pot.

5. Add just enough water to cover the ingredients. Cover the pot.

6. Bring this to a boil and simmer 3 or 4 hours. Stir now and then and add more water if needed.

7. THE ADULT REMOVES the ham shank to cool. Cut up the meat in bite-size pieces.

8. If you wish, it is good to smash some of the beans with the food mill.

This is delicious served with warm corn bread.

Pizza—Yummy and Fun!

You Need:

1 pound hamburger or pork sausage or Italian sausage

1 large or 2 medium onions

1 15-ounce can tomato sauce

1 6-ounce can tomato paste

1/2 t. (scant) oregano

1/2 t. (scant) pepper

8 ounces grated cheddar cheese or cheese of your choice

3 cans (10 biscuits per can) refrigerator biscuits

Yields: 30 small, delicious pizzas

How To:

1. The children help chop the onions as suggested under Vegetable Beef Soup, How To steps 2 and 3.

2. THE ADULT browns the meat and chopped onions together, drains and discards all grease.

3. Stir together in a bowl the meat-onion mixture, tomato sauce and paste, oregano, and pepper.

4. Lightly grease three large cookie sheets. My cookie sheets measure 15 by12 inches.

5. The children and adults work together to flatten the biscuits on the cookie sheets, put some of the tomato mixture in the middle of each biscuit, (spread toward the edge but try to keep a rim of plain crust), and sprinkle on the grated cheese.

6. Bake at 400 degrees until brown—maybe 8 to 10 minutes. *Serve with a salad for a wonderful meal.*

Did you notice? The ingredients in the pizza include 4 of the basic food groups.

Dirt Cake—Delicious Served Out of a New Plastic Flower Pot with a New Small Garden Trowel

This is really fun, good, and a great conversation starter.

You Need:

1 8-inch diameter new plastic flower pot washed and dried

1 new garden trowel or spoon if you prefer

20-ounce package of oreo cookies

1/2 stick margarine at room temperature

1 8-ounce package cream cheese at room temperature

1 cup sifted powdered sugar

3 1/2 cups milk

2 packages French vanilla instant pudding (don't substitute regular vanilla), 3.4-ounce size

1 12-ounce container of Cool Whip

How To:

1. Separate 1 oreo cookie and save 1/2 of it to cover the hole in the flower pot.

2. Crumble the oreo cookies with a blender or rolling pin. Children will enjoy using a rolling pin. It will work to put a few cookies at a time in a plastic bag for smashing and rolling. The icing makes the crumbs stick to the sides of the bag, but they can be rubbed free with clean fingers.

3. Set cookie crumbs aside.

Steps 4 and 6 are AN ADULT or an older child's job:

4. With an electric mixer mix the margarine, cream cheese, and powdered sugar.

5. In another bowl mix pudding, milk, and cool whip.

6. Combine the 2 mixtures from steps 4 and 5 and mix well.

7. Cover the hole in the bottom of your flower pot with the cookie half.

8. Alternate cookie crumbs and pudding mixture in layers in the pot, beginning and ending with the cookie crumbs.

9. Stick in a plastic flower for the finishing touch.

10. Refrigerate until ready to serve.

 Now you are ready to serve your guests or family or class your delicious dirt cake.

Playdough

These are DO NOT EAT recipes.

 Children love to squeeze, roll, punch, and form playdough into many wonderful shapes. Try both recipes to find your favorite playdough.

COOKED PLAYDOUGH (my favorite)

You Need:

3 cups flour

1 1/2 cups salt

2 T. cream of tarter (important—do not omit)

3 T. oil (any cooking oil)

3 cups water

Few drops food color (optional)

How To:

1. Divide up the measuring jobs among the adults and children. See Helpful Hints 8 and 9 on page 180. In a classroom, nine children could each measure 1/3 cup of flour to make your 3 cup total. Do the same with salt and so on so everyone has a turn.

2. Put all the dry ingredients into a heavy pot.

3. Add the wet ingredients gradually, with everyone taking turns stirring. (This is not easy.) Try to get it smooth but don't worry if you have some lumps.

4. THE ADULT cooks the mixture, *stirring constantly,* until it clumps together.

5. Dump the clump of warm playdough onto a formica surface.

6. While it is still warm, divide the dough among all the people and *have fun kneading it.*

It feels so good, and the more you knead it the smoother it gets!

Store in an air-tight container.

Use and reuse. It keeps for months.

UNCOOKED PLAYDOUGH

You Need:

Full Recipe	1/3 Recipe
3 cups flour	1 cup flour
1 cup salt	1/3 cup salt
2 T. oil	2 t. oil
1 cup water	1/3 cup water

How To:

Use your hands to mix everything together. Work with the dough until it all clumps together. Then knead it for smoothness.

Store in an air-tight container.

The 1/3 recipe may be used if each person wants to mix her or his very own playdough.

Store in a pint-size, air-tight zipper bag or any airtight container.

Isn't making playdough fun? 😊

Index